www.ingramcontent.com/pod-product-compliance
Lightning Source LLC
Chambersburg PA
CBHW042016150426
43197CB00002B/49

9 7 8 4 9 0 7 0 0 9 1 2 0

Carbon Shinai
カーボンシナイ

- CF-Type
- DB-Type
- K1-Type
- K2-Type

Orange   Red   Yellow

The official Carbon Shinai rubber stopper have been improved.

The NEW official rubber stopper
¥300 (Domestic price in Japan)

WARNING!! Never use anything other than our official rubber stopper on your Carbon Shinai !!

When in use of your Carbon Shinai.....

1. To prevent injury, be sure to use our official rubber stopper. Do not use stoppers made for conventional bamboo shinai on your Carbon Shinai, as there is a risk of injury to your opponents if the tip distorts or the piece of shinai slips out from the rubber stopper and penetrates through their men-gane. (men grill)

2. When choosing a saki-gawa (tip leather), make sure that it is more than 5cm in length and completely covers the official rubber stopper. If the saki-gawa is shorter than 5cm, there is a risk of injury to your opponents if the piece of shinai slips out and penetrates their men-gane.

3. Whatever the reason, do not shave the surface or cut the length of your Carbon Shinai. If you shave or cut, the Carbon Shinai will get damaged to result in injury to your opponents.

4. Always check the condition of the surface of your Carbon Shinai before, during and after use. As soon as you notice any damage, stop use of the shinai immediately. There is a danger of injury to your opponents if your Carbon Shinai gets split or broken.

5. When tying the naka-yui (leather binding), either tie a knot in the tsuru-ito (cord), or tie one end of the naka-yui to the tsuru-ito, or by another means ensuring that it does not move up and down during use. If there is any damage whatsoever to the saki-gawa, tsuka-gawa (hilt), rubber stopper, tsuru-ito and so on, replace them immediately with new ones.

6. If the tip of the Carbon Shinai get damaged, or a slat is protruding out of the saki-gawa, there is a danger that it could penetrate your opponent's men-gane and injure them.

Kendogu Revolution

Mu-Jun Men
武楯面

WARNING!!

1. Under no circumstances should organic solvents (such as thinner, alcohol, benzene, toluene, acetone, gasoline, kerosene, etc.), acidic or alkali chemicals, domestic cleansers, car cleansers, or anti-mist sprays, be used to clean the shield. These substances will cause the shield to deteriorate, leading to clouding, cracking or breaking, thereby resulting in danger of injury to the face.

2. Should the shield develop deep scratches or cracks on either the outer or inner surface, discontinue use of the shield immediately, and replace it with an undamaged shield. If the shield is used in such a condition, there is a danger of its breaking, causing injury to the face.

3. It should be fully understood that, as with the traditional Japanese Kendo-Men (mask), there is still the danger of injury to the face through fragments of broken bamboo or Carbon Shinai pieces penetrating through areas not covered by the shield.

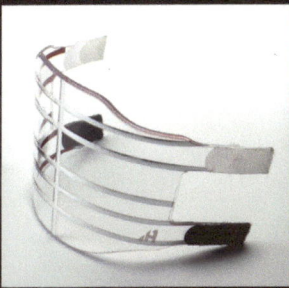
SG-Type

- SCIENCE TO SEEK SAFETY -

HASEGAWA
HASEGAWA CORPORATION

WEB : http://kendo.hasegawakagaku.co.jp/
Email : contact@hasegawakagaku.co.jp

Carbon Shinai — Points to be checked

DANGER !! **ATTENTION !!**

Before these happen.....

Although the Carbon Shinai is much more durable than conventional bamboo ones, it will inevitably be broken since it is a Kendo sword which is beaten hard and thrust over and over again. Inspect the condition of the surface, sides or reverse of the Shinai's pieces before, during and after use, and stop use of the Carbon Shinai immediately should the damage like the following pictures be observed. (The pictures are just one examples of many.)

- Damage on the surface

- An unglued surface sheet

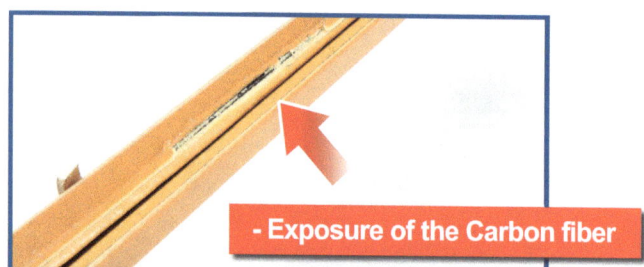
- Exposure of the Carbon fiber

- Longitudinal crack on the surface

- Damage and ungluing of the surface

- Crack on the reverse

There is a case that the reverse gets cracked even without any damage on the surface. Inspect the inside of the Shinai by pushing pieces with fingers unbinding the Naka-yui.

HASEGAWA-KOTE

- Detachable and washable "Tenouchi" is easy to wash and dry.
- "Tenouchi" is replaceable when it torn. No need to repair.

Kote (Main part)

Tenouchi (Inner)

- SCIENCE TO SEEK SAFETY -
HASEGAWA

HASEGAWA CORPORATION
http://kendo.hasegawakagaku.co.jp/

What is Tornado-stitch®?

- Innovative patented design
- Enhanced protection

- Correct angle of strike immediately visible
- Perfect for Kendo instructors

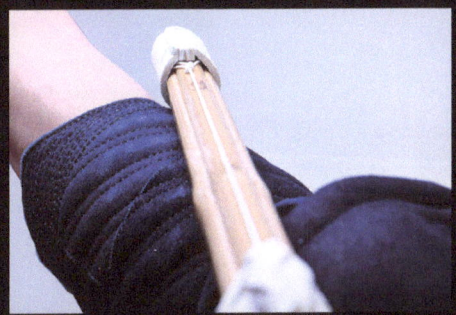

- Improved wrist mobility
- Available in indigo-dyed deerskin and orizashi cotton.

Read the whole story about the Tornado Stitch® and see our interview with the All Japan Kendo Federation Vice President, Mr. Fukumoto Shuji, about the advantages of the Tozando Tornado Stitch® Kote at www.Tozandoshop.com

Tornado-stitch® (Patent pending 2014-4504)

Tornado-stitch Indigo-dyed deerskin model

Tornado-stitch Orizashi model

Tornado-stitch®, recommended for instructors, true to the essence of Kendo

The Shinai is a Sword. When you think of it like that, the concept of "Hasuji" becomes clear. "To strike with spirit, using the correct posture, hitting the target with the correct "Hasuji", following through with proper Zanshin". This is what is stated in the All Japan Kendo Federation Shiai and Referee Regulations. Also, "To strike with Spirit, Sword and Body as one", this is something that anyone practicing Kendo has to strive for while

Being aware of this, we listened to the voices of kendo instructors. They would ask for a Bogu that would perfectly protect when hit, while being exceptionally durable - all this would make teaching the correct Hasuji and playing Motodachi easier for them. To answer these requests, we kept researching and developing the possibilities for years, going through several prototypes in the process. As a result, by radically modifying the stitching method, we finally managed to create a unique Kote-buton, excellent in absorbing impact. The Tozando Tornado-stitch® was born.

We got an opportunity to show this innovative Kote to Mr. Fukumoto, the vice president of the All Japan Kendo Federation. "To be able to strike with the correct angle, this is the most important and critical difference of these Kote". These Kote both teach the essence of Kendo, making it easy to understand the concept of the sword`s "Hasuji", and allow the instructor to receive the strikes safely.

The Tornado-stitch® Kote are made in our factory in Iwate prefecture under strict quality requirements. They are made by our craftsmen, who use all of their skills and heart, to make them one of the few "Made in Japan" Kote left on the market today. We are certain that these Tornado-stitch® Kote, used and loved by many Kenshi around the world, will become a true pillar of the promotion and the diffusion of strong and correct Kendo.

Tozando Co.,Ltd.
www.tozando.com

KENDO WORLD Volume 7.1 December 2013 Contents

Editorial _____ 2

The Features of Kendo and My Experience
Takeyasu Yoshimitsu (FIK President and AJKF Supreme Advisor) _ 4

Making the grade: Roberto Kishikawa on passing the 8-dan examination _____ 7

The 61st All Japan Kendo Championships __ 14

Hanshi Says Nakano Makoto (Hanshi 8-dan) _____ 16

Grading Successfully: Part 1
Shigematsu Kimiaki (Kyoshi 8-dan) _____ 18

The Nuts 'n' Bolts of Kendo
Waza Training _____ 28

Reidan-jichi Part 16 **Kihon Dōsa** No. 5 _____ 31

sWords of Wisdom **"Mumyō wo kiru"** _____ 34

Bujutsu Jargon Part 5 _____ 36

Why Am I Alive? Ogawa Chūtarō _____ 38

Unlocking Japan: Part 25
Oh the Shame _____ 39

Green Budo _____ 40

The 2nd World Combat Games _____ 43

Meiji Shrine Kobudō Demonstrations __ 45

The 10th ASEAN Kendo Tournament
—Taikai Report _____ 49

Looking at the History and Future of Japanese Women's Kendo _____ 52

Kendo That Cultivates People
Part 15: Teaching Kendo to the Next Generation (Part 1) _____ 57

Book Mark
Kendo, Inherited Wisdom and Personal Reflections _____ 63

The Kendo Coach: Sports Psychology in Kendo
Part 10—Series Summary _____ 64

Tachikiri _____ 70

A Comparative Analysis of Bushido and Chivalry
—Part Two _____ 73

It's Academic:
Notes from the Japanese Academy of Budo _ 77

Electromyographic patterns during kendo hiki-waza strikes in kendoka of different experience _____ 79

Mario Bottoni's Legacy _____ 84

Shinai Sagas **The Coil** _____ 85

Confusion Regarding Waza Among Beginner Kendoka _____ 88

NITO PART 7: Practical Techniques _____ 91

Martial AIDS
The Shoe/Kote Dryer _____ 99

Kendo World Staff
- Bunkasha International President & Editor-in-Chief— Alex Bennett PhD
- Bunkasha International Vice President & Assistant Editor— Michael Ishimatsu-Prime MA
- Bunkasha International Vice President & Graphic Design— Shishikura 'Kan' Masashi
- Bunkasha International Vice President— Hamish Robison
- Bunkasha International Vice President— Michael Komoto MA
- Bunkasha International General Manager— Baptiste Tavernier MA
- Senior Consultant— Yonemoto Masayuki

KW Staff Writers / Translators / Photographers / Graphic Designer / Sub-editors
- Axel Pilgrim PhD
- Blake Bennett MA
- Bruce Flanagan MA
- Bryan Peterson
- Charlie Kondek
- Gabriel Weitzner
- Honda Sōtarō PhD
- Imafuji Masahiro MBA
- Jeff Broderick
- Kate Sylvester MA
- Lockie Jackson PhD
- Miho Maki
- Paul Benson
- Scott Huegel (MaSC)
- Sergio Boffa PhD
- Stephen Nagy PhD
- Steven Harwood MA
- Stuart Gibson
- Taylor Winter
- Tony Cundy
- Trevor Jones
- Tyler Rothmar
- Yamaguchi Remi
- Vivian Yung

KW would like to thank the following people and organisations for their valuable cooperation:
- All Japan Kendo Federation
- Chiba Budo-gu
- Hasegawa Teiichi - President, Hasegawa Corporation
- *Kendo Jidai* Magazine
- *Kendo Nihon* Magazine
- Nippon Budokan Foundation
- TOZANDO

Guest Writers
- Donatella Castelli (TOZANDO staff member; Kendo 6-dan)
- Graham Sayer (President of the New Zealand Kendo Federation)
- Jonathan Levine-Ogura (School teacher in Iwate Prefecture; Kendo 5-dan)
- Roberto Kishikawa (Kendo 8-dan)
- Manuela Hoflehner (Captain of the Austrian Women's Kendo Team)
- Nakano Makoto (Kendo Hanshi 8-dan)
- Nakano Yasoji (Now deceased. Kendo Hanshi 9-dan)
- Ōya Minoru (Prof. International Budo University; Kendo Kyōshi 7-dan)
- Ozawa Hiroshi (Kendo Kyōshi 8-dan)
- Roberto Kishikawa (Kendo 8-dan)
- Ryan McIntyre (Student at Victoria University, Wellington)
- Shigematsu Kimiaki (Kendo Kyōshi 8-dan)
- Sumi Masatake (Kendo Hanshi 8-dan)
- Takeyasu Yoshimitsu (FIK President and AJKF Supreme Advisor)
- Thomas Sluyter (Renshinjuku Kendo Dojo)
- Yamaguchi Masato (Nitō practitioner)
- Yotani K. & Maesaka S. (Faculty members at National Institute of Fitness and Sports in Kanoya)

COPYRIGHT 2013 Bunkasha International Corporation. No part of this publication may be reproduced in any form whatsoever without written permission from the publisher, except by writers who are permitted to quote brief passages for the purpose of review or reference. Kindly contact Bunkasha International Corporation at info@kendo-world.com.

Editorial Conventions Used in KW Inevitably in a magazine of this nature, many non-English words appear in the text. All Japanese words are italicised and include macrons (ū, ō) etc., apart from common place names and nouns, and words in some captions and headings. As a general exception, KW treats all the martial arts (budo), such as kendo, iaido, jodo, ranks, and so on as Anglicised words without using macrons. Japanese names are written in accordance to the traditional Japanese manner of family name followed by given name. Traditional *ryûha* are written with capitals and therefore are not italicised. 'Kata' with a capital 'K' refers to the set of Nippon Kendo Kata, and *kata* refers to set forms in general. The masculine personal pronoun is used throughout the text in some articles in the interest of readability, and is in no way meant to slight the significant contributions made by female kendoka.

Editorial
The Times, They are a-Changin'
By Alex Bennett

This is *Kendo World*'s 25th edition. We began publishing in 2001, and we thank you for your continued support over the years. Hamish Robison and I started the magazine on a whim after watching the All Japan Kendo Championships on TV at Lockie Jackson's apartment in Osaka. At the time, there was virtually nothing available on the web or in book form that could satisfy the ravenous needs of budding kendoka around the world. Those of us lucky enough to be in Japan would diligently make a VHS of the champs from the NHK coverage, and send it back home to do the dojo rounds. That was only a decade ago!

We had no idea about the publishing industry, or how to put a magazine or a website together, but as the beers flowed, the concept started to grow. It even seemed like a good idea the next morning as we nursed our hangovers. This was the decider, and proof that we needed to follow through. The blind leading the blind, our driving force was our love of kendo. Looking back, it is a miracle of sorts that we have managed to continue. To be honest, there have been some grim times for KW over the years and sometimes we wondered what it was all for—on occasion it seemed like such a thankless task. We made more than our fair share of errors in judgement as well, but like any kendo training, though, the secret is to keep getting back up and stuck in to the task at hand. Never say die!

The magazine continues to evolve, and now we have a fantastic team working hard on each issue. Our mission remains the same: to provide the international kendo community with reliable and useful information to facilitate a deeper understanding of the essence of kendo and its related arts. With the internet and the simplification of publishing technology, there is now an abundance of information on kendo available to the international kendo community. Some of it is good, and some is not so reliable. Testament to the quality of KW's content, however, came with a rather gratifying, but odd phone call from the All Japan Kendo Federation recently. They asked us to be an "official collaborating company". I am not exactly sure what this means, but will take it as an indication that our hard work over the years is being recognised as making a contribution to kendo culture.

On that starting note, for this editorial I decided to take a serious look at a transition in the perception of budo in Japan since the inception of this magazine. There are many topics that I could have covered here, such as the incredible elevation of the level of world kendo over the last decade, but I will save that for another day. The problem of budo and violence has been a simmering hotpot of broth set to boil over and stain the stove in the last ten years in Japan, and I would like to address this rather sombre topic here instead.

As a bleak counterbalance to the euphoria experienced with Tokyo's successful 2020 Olympic bid, Japan's sports world has been rocked by a number of scandals of late. In particular, bullying and violent behaviour by instructors towards their charges in schools, universities, and national teams has been a disturbing feature, and underlies a sinister 'culture of abuse' rampant in the strict hierarchical relationships that characterise sports clubs in Japanese schools.

That is not to say that violence in sports is a new phenomenon in Japan. Simply, the Japanese media, always in search of a juicy morsel to chew on, has turned its attention to the problem with apparent sanctimonious glee in recent times. Although by no means the only culprit, judo has been at the forefront of media bashing. Kendo also gets the odd inglorious feature spot on the TV, too. I am left wondering, "Why now?"

A remarkably little known fact in Japan is the number of deaths at schools through judo in the last three decades, something that has been highlighted in an article published in the *Japan Times*. "Over the 27-year period between 1983 and 2009, 108 students aged 12 to 17 died as a result of judo accidents in Japanese schools, an average of four a year", which is "more than five times higher than in any other sport. About 65 per cent of these fatalities came from brain injuries. This is clear evidence of a dangerous trend in Japanese schools." (*Japan Times*, August 26, 2010.) Apart from the horrendous number of deaths of young people, the fact that not a single person has been held responsible by the law in any of the fatalities is astounding.

Still, it is the media and public that place high expectations on national team members to win as a matter of national pride, and parents entrust their children to teachers to discipline them and get results in their respective sports. The coaches are products of a long-entrenched system and mindset, and the immense pressures placed upon them to get results makes them even more set in their ways. There is a thin line between the good old rigorous *keiko* session where the sensei pushes students beyond their physical and mental limits, and physical and mental abuse pure and simple. Until now, most have turned a blind eye to excessive cruelty in the dojo.

Judo in Japan seems to be idealistically discombobulated. As a competitive sport, it has lost its purity and attractiveness, and as a means for education, it is contradictory and arguably angles towards breeding contempt and egotism. The problems in judo in Japan coming to the fore now are endemic, and it will take nothing more than a massive paradigm shift to re-establish judo's latent worth as a competitive sport, and as a vehicle for personal growth—where its much heralded value lies.

I was asked to interpret for two distinguished non-Japanese judo authorities on this very subject in Japan recently. Michel Brousse-sensei, vice president of the Fédération Française de Judo et Disciplines Associées (French Federation of Judo and Related Disciplines), and Mike Callan-sensei, chief executive of Judospace Educational Institute. They gave lectures titled "Dangerous Judo or Dangerous Coaching?" and "Judo Injuries in Children: A Coach Education Solution?" respectively at the invitation of judo legend Yamashita Yasuhiro-sensei, current VP of the All Japan Judo Federation, and founder of the Solidarity of International Judo Education NPO. Sponsored by the Ministry of Foreign Affairs, I found it fascinating that the Japanese government and judo world in Japan would call upon non-Japanese to give them advice on how they can get back to the traditional educational ideals on which judo was founded, and look for ways to eradicate the tragic accidents that mar this important culture. I applaud Professor Yamashita's efforts to clean up Japanese judo so forthrightly.

It got me thinking a lot about the changing face of kendo in Japan over the last decade or so, since *Kendo World*'s inception. My induction into the world of kendo at a Japanese high school by today's standards was… let me just say it was pure hell. But then, it was because of this severe regime of torment and perdition through a daily diet of fear and trepidation that I discovered an inner strength I did not even know existed. I was able to tap into a side of me that only the fiercest of 'prodding' could make me aware of. I am eternally grateful for the experience. It is what got me hooked on kendo.

Being involved with college kendo now, and also high school kendo to a much lesser extent, I have noticed a distinct move away from the excessively demanding training sessions and regimented club life. Of course, there is considerable disparity between institutions, but gone are the days now when drinking water during training is an unthinkable corruption of the kendo spirit. Regular water intake is encouraged now because of recognition of the dangers of dehydration, especially in the severely humid Japanese summer months. In fact, most of the deaths that occur in kendo are the result of heat exhaustion. Such is the level of concern, the All Japan Kendo Federation has a detailed section on their HP on how to avoid and treat heat exhaustion.

Then there is the hazing in university clubs. Even though they are under aged, forcing freshmen to drink copious amounts of alcohol at club drinking parties has also been greatly reduced. When I was a student at a Japanese university, ambulance callouts for alcohol poisoning were not only a common occurrence, it was almost considered a matter of pride. Fortunately, this irresponsible 'tradition' has been virtually snuffed out by universities who are terrified of the imminent media reaction when drunken students get out of hand, not to mention the dangers to student health. This practice also gave rise to a new bad word in Japan—"*aru-hara*" (alcohol harassment).

Next are the changes in actual *keiko* methodology and attitudes. The line between hard training and violent training is sometimes difficult to distinguish. (This subject has been masterfully analysed by Blake Bennett in his recent series of articles in *Kendo World*, the last of which is in this issue.) A certain amount of harsh training and discipline is, I believe, absolutely vital in kendo to forge the physical and mental strength needed to prevail in times of adversity, be it in the dojo, *shiai-jō*, or by extension, life in general.

Nevertheless, with the much-publicised incidents of bullying and violence in sports clubs in Japan, the tolerance for 'questionable' or overzealous teaching practices to elicit discipline and fighting spirit is diminishing because of finger-pointing parents, paranoid headmasters, nervous education boards, and students or kohai who are becoming more vociferous in their accusations of victimization. I am reminded of a very recent incident in which a junior student at a prestigious kendo university complained of bullying and unnecessarily violent 'instruction' at the hands of his sempai. To be honest, I have heard of, seen, and been involved in a lot worse in my kendo career, but the fact that the university in question decided to pull out of the National Championships as a result, is a clear indication of a paradigm shift in kendo attitudes.

Instructors brought up in the traditional, ruthless 'kendo spirit overcomes all' training mentality are at a loss. Kendo teachers and senior practitioners are finding themselves in a swirling tide of changing social attitudes towards what are considered acceptable educational practices, and are having to adjust accordingly. Of course, this is surely a good thing, but I wonder if the massive pendulum swing in the opposite direction will not result in a watering down of kendo's essence.

I believe balance and common sense is always going to be the key, as well as a clear understanding of what we are trying to achieve or accomplish through doing kendo. It is natural for culture to evolve, and change is more desirable than being stuck in the nebulous quagmire of the 'bonds of tradition' simply for tradition's sake; but certainly not all aspects of tradition are bad. The word "*keiko*" used to describe training in budo comes from the idiom "*keiko-shōkon*" (think about the ways of the ancients to illuminate the present). In other words, as kendo practitioners, it is important to contemplate and identify the fundamental nature of budo and its traditions, its quintessence, and apply it to our lives today.

It has to be relevant to our existence in modern society, and change should be embraced for this purpose; but let us not throw the baby out with the bath water…

The Features of Kendo and My Experience

Takeyasu Yoshimitsu

FIK President and AJKF Supreme Advisor

Congratulations to *Kendo World* on the publication of their 25th edition. I was asked to write a greeting in the very first issue of *Kendo World* in 2001 in my capacity as the president of the All Japan Kendo Federation (AJKF). I retired from that position this year, but still serve kendo as the president of the International Kendo Federation (FIK) and as the supreme advisor to the AJKF. I am happy to see that *Kendo World* continues to provide information about kendo to the international kendo community.

I would like to take this opportunity to introduce the process in which modern kendo evolved, and its various characteristics. The techniques of kendo derive from combat with Japanese swords. As a weapon, the Japanese sword, commonly known as the *katana*, played a significant role in the old battlefields of Japan. Many schools or traditions specialising in sword techniques emerged. The martial art of swordsmanship was referred to as "*kenjutsu*" (techniques of the sword). Schools developed set patterns of technical sequences called "*kata*" in which the secret techniques of the school were memorised and passed on to ensuing generations of disciples.

Japan was unified under a nationwide feudal system from the seventeenth century, and social stability and peace prevailed. By this stage, firearms had already been imported from the West, and the role of the *katana* on the battlefield was diminished. Still, the Japanese sword became symbolic of samurai status and the warrior class, but the practice of swordsmanship through "*kata*" with replica wooden swords gradually went into decline because of this peace.

In Edo, which is now modern day Tokyo, bamboo was used in the creation of practice swords known as "*shinai*" that replaced the more dangerous wooden ones. This enabled practitioners to train in the techniques of *kenjutsu* by participating in full-contact fencing bouts utilising protective training equipment where they could strike or be struck without fear of injury. The development of this training equipment made use of craft skills already perfected to make traditional battle armour and helmets.

It was quickly realised that fencing in this way was quite exhilarating, and also provided a means for ascetic training. The striking targets in fencing bouts were set at the head ("*men*"), wrists ("*kote*"), torso ("*dō*"), and thrusts to the throat ("*tsuki*"). In order to encourage practitioners to train hard, it was necessary to create a system in which winners and losers could be decided. Adhering to established methods of wielding a Japanese sword with its peculiar curved shape and singular cutting edge with ridges on each side of the blade, the angle of the cutting edge on impact was also an important consideration when deciding a point in a match even with the cylindrical bamboo *shinai*. Other aspects of traditional swordsmanship were also incorporated into the new competitive form. Furthermore, the psychological essentials cultivated among samurai through the study of traditional swordsmanship and other elements were assimilated as the new form of *shinai-kenjutsu* was systemised throughout the eighteenth century.

Kenjutsu was originally only studied by the samurai class, but broke away from being techniques solely for combat into an exciting competitive pursuit that spread to the masses. In today's terms, the advent of *shinai-kenjutsu* could be considered as the realisation of a great innovation.

In the mid-eighteenth century, Japan underwent a massive political transformation as it became a modern nation state. *Shinai-kenjutsu* transcended all class boundaries and became increasingly popular. It was recognized that training in *kenjutsu* would be useful for strengthening the minds and bodies of children, and it was thus introduced into the school system making it even more widespread. Until this point, *kenjutsu* had simply been a contest in which

combatants tried to defeat each other. However, it eventually became recognised as a means for spiritual growth, and then as a way of instilling morality. In other words, it evolved into a "way" or "path" that practitioners walked throughout their lives as they sought self-perfection. This is when *kenjutsu* (the techniques of the sword) was changed in name to "kendo", which literally means the "Way" of the sword.

Shinai-kendo, in which competitors fence each other in matches, retains many of the same elements as other sports, and its competitive side is attractive for many practitioners. Nevertheless, kendo is promoted not merely as a sport for gaining victory in competition,

but as a vehicle to "develop one's humanity" through training. The goal of the AJKF's activities is to "Encourage personal development, and to contribute to society". There are few injuries or accidents, and it can be practised by old and young alike. The equipment is very elegant and refined. There is also a "*dan*" or rank system that serves as proof of technical proficiency, and a "*shōgō*" title system awarded in recognition of the experienced practitioner's character and insight. Examinations for both of these accreditations are strict and impartial. Matches are adjudicated fairly in accordance with the "Match and Referee Regulations". There are universities that train specialist teachers, as well as the AJKF's many seminar events designed to enhance the level and understanding of instructors. Kendo can be practised together by people from all walks of life, regardless of age or gender.

I started kendo when I was 12 years old. I trained hard throughout my childhood right up until I graduated from university. I had to stop during the war years, but was able to pick it up again by joining some active groups where I could train a few times a week from around 1960. Now I train once a week, so my kendo career spans over 80 years, and I still feel great.

I would like to mention one of my recent experiences. In the prewar school system, kendo was popular at high schools and vocational schools. The school system was changed after the war, but those of us who practised kendo before got together again, and decided to hold a tournament representing the old schools that we went to. The first tournament was held in 1975, and it continued for many years. As the participants were all in their eighties, however, the last was the 36th tournament, which was held in 2010. I am very lucky that I was healthy, and able to help organise the event each year. I participated in all of them, proudly representing my old school. It made me feel the great benefits of studying kendo.

The FIK was started in 1970 and now has 52 affiliates around the world, with the World Kendo Championships (WKC) being staged every three years. The 16th WKC will be held in 2015 at the Nippon Budokan in Tokyo, and we are very much looking forward to welcoming the world's top kendo practitioners to Japan for this event.

MAKING THE GRADE
ROBERTO KISHIKAWA
on passing the 8-dan examination

Interview with Roberto Kishikawa-sensei, 8-dan
November 29, 2013
Interviewer: Dr. Stephen R. Nagy
       Chinese University of Hong Kong
Photos by Chester Ong

NOVEMBER 27, 2013, marks an important date for kendoka around the world. That early evening, Roberto Kishikawa, a Brazilian national and permanent resident of Hong Kong, was promoted to 8-dan by the All Japan Kendo Federation (AJKF). As the first non-Japanese national to pass the 8-dan grading in Japan, Kishikawa-sensei has excited and inspired the overseas kendo community to strive for the highest levels of kendo. What follows is an interview with Kishikawa-sensei concerning his exam experience, views on kendo, and journey to 8-dan.

NAGY: Congratulations on your achievement! As you know, there are only a handful of people outside of Japan who have received their 8-dan in Japan, but they are all Japanese nationals who were born and raised in Japan.

KISHIKAWA-SENSEI: Yes, up until now the only people promoted to 8-dan have been Japanese.

NAGY: As the first non-Japanese who has passed the 8-dan exam in Japan, what kind of responsibilities or feelings do you have?

KISHIKAWA-SENSEI: First of all, it was a big surprise for me. As we discussed over the past few years, we should always try to challenge ourselves and I took the test with that spirit. To be candid, I didn't really have confidence I could pass, but at the very same time it is very satisfying that all my training up to now has been in the right direction.

After being promoted to 8-dan, as a kenshi, and as one who is also not Japanese, I think that a new road has been laid for kendoka around the world to strive for and achieve their kendo goals. Many of my friends from around the world whom I competed against in the world championships and other tournaments that are already 7-dan, congratulated me, but they also expressed to me that they are inspired to practise even harder.

I think that the world kendo community has been moved by this achievement, and it is echoing throughout it so that many people will start to challenge 8-dan earlier. As the first 8-dan who was not born and raised in Japan, I think that I have a responsibility to show what we need to do next.

That being said, I should be clear that 8-dan is not the final target. Actually, I am already trying to discover

what to do next. Having only just passed 8-dan [two days before], I cannot see the next peak or goal. At this moment, I can see where I have been in terms of my kendo journey, but I cannot see the following step. It is still unclear, but one of the things I need to find is a good direction for kendo, not only internationally, but also in Japan. I think this is also my responsibility.

NAGY: Many of my kendo friends around the world know that you have been my kendo teacher in Hong Kong. They asked me about your kendo background, major influences, teachers, and what in your kendo background enabled you to achieve 8-dan.

KISHIKAWA-SENSEI: I started kendo in Brazil when I was five years old. At that time I started with my brother. At the age of five, we did a competition style of kendo. In the Brazilian kendo community at that time *kihon* was not really emphasised in *keiko*. We just enjoyed fighting each other. So for me, that was kendo in the beginning. Also, my father played a role in my kendo. He always pushed my brother and me to get good results. We thought of competition as "life or death", because if you wanted to survive in competition, you had to have a matching attitude. I have had this kind of mentality since I was a kid.

I won my first championship when I was 10 years old, the Brazilian tournament. In fact, we have five tournaments a year and I won all five. In 1980, the Youth World

Kendo tournament was held in Hawaii, and that was my first international competition. Unfortunately, at that time the Brazilian team didn't win or get a good result, but it was an excellent experience to help me and other Brazilians to prepare for the next tournament as I could grasp what the level of kendo in the world was. This boosted my interest in fighting on the international stage.

I have won many Brazilian tournaments, but I cannot remember the actual number. I was five-time Brazilian champion and Sao Paolo State champion. On the world stage, my first appearance was in 1985 at the 6th World Kendo Championships (WKC). The Brazilian team came 2nd and I competed as Fukushō and Taishō. I received the Fighting Spirit award in the individual competition. The next tournament was in Korea in 1988. Brazil came 3rd and I was in the top eight in the individuals. I also received the Fighting Spirit award again. Brazil did not place in 1991 in Canada. In 1994 in France, I received two Fighting Spirit awards in the individual and team matches. 1997 was my last tournament for Brazil as Taishō, and again I received the Fighting Spirit award. After that, I decided to leave the tournament side of kendo to search more for the real kendo, to try to understand what kendo really was. That was the point where my kendo life took a different direction. I think that the new path combined with my competition experience contributed to me achieving 8-dan.

Nagy: So it was the transition from a more sport- oriented kendo to the philosophical side of kendo that was important in achieving your goal?

Kishikawa-sensei: Yes. Not only is fighting and technique important to kendo development, but I also believe that we must explore *seme, maai*, and the psychological aspects of kendo to really discover its deeper side. We need to learn this to fight our opponent psychologically, not just physically.

Nagy: Kendoka around the world are very interested in this kind of kendo. Did you have teachers or experiences that led you in this direction, or was it mostly through your own training?

Kishikawa-sensei: In my kendo career, my sensei have given me a lot of advice. It isn't as if someone said something and everything changed. Rather, I think it was a combination of my interests to try and find a deeper side of kendo and the fact that I was lucky to have many excellent instructors who gave me very good kendo-related advice.

This is true not only during this initial period, but even now in Hong Kong. We have many high-ranking sensei visiting Hong Kong, and I have plenty of opportunities to visit Japan and meet other teachers. Listening to their words and thinking about what they said really had an impact on my kendo and helped me find a way forward.

Nagy: When did you live in Japan? Where did you train?

Kishikawa-sensei: I lived in Japan from about 1990 to 1998, for almost 10 years. In the beginning, I trained at Yokohama National University (YNU) as a student. I was a MEXT scholarship recipient, allowing me to study at Yokohama National University for my MA. I was able to practise at the university dojo as a student. The university was also in Kanagawa, so I was able to practise with the Kanagawa police force as well.

My training frequency decreased a lot when I started work at Hitachi. Most of my training was in the weekend. I went to YNU, Kokushikan University and Obukan (Sakurai-sensei's private dojo). These were the dojo where I did most of my training while in Japan.

Nagy: When did you move to Hong Kong?

Kishikawa-sensei: In 2002.

Nagy: I think one of the biggest barriers for many foreign kendoka when they move back to their home countries is the lack of high-ranking practitioners to train with. How did you overcome this?

Kishikawa-sensei: Indeed. When I arrived in Hong Kong in 2002, I was the first 7-dan, and Horibe-sensei had just received his 7-dan. Except for us two, most of the teachers were 4-dan and 5-dan. Also, the young players' level was quite low. In the beginning, it was a big challenge to conduct *keiko* and not lose my direction in that environment.

On the other hand, Hong Kong is very close to Japan and we have regular visits of Japanese teachers such as Inoue-sensei from Nara, Sumi-sensei from Fukuoka, Chiba-sensei from Tokyo, Furukawa-sensei from Hokkaido, Iwadate-sensei from Chiba, and Itō-sensei from Tokyo for kendo and iaido.

My point is that relationships and *shugyō* can be conducted with many famous sensei because we live in Hong Kong. These kind of relationships helped me get good tips and advice to advance my direction in kendo. Now after 11 years in Hong Kong, we have seven or eight 7-dan and many 6-dan, and I am also coaching the Hong

Kong national team. When I started teaching, most of the players were *shodan* or 2-dan, but now they are 4-dan and 5-dan and their skills have improved a lot. The kind of environment that we have now is different, and that has also contributed to my success.

NAGY: It's a big challenge as most that pass the 8-dan exam are in fact professional kendoka. They work at the police stations and their full time jobs are in fact kendo. In your case, you balanced a full time job and family obligations, and still managed to pass the exam.

KISHIKAWA-SENSEI: That's true. You have to balance work, family, and kendo. Outside Japan (both in the work and cultural context) there is no such thing as a professional kendoka. As foreign kendoka we have many hurdles to overcome to achieve those elusive upper ranks, including of all the technical hurdles.

NAGY: Can you offer three suggestions for foreign kendoka preparing for their 7-dan or 8-dan grading?

KISHIKAWA-SENSEI: First of all, we must keep in mind our own history, our origins and what we have learned until now from many sensei. Who you are now represents your collective kendo experience, and all the people you have met. I believe that we must treat these encounters as something very precious. I also believe very strongly that we should keep in our minds who we are now, because we have had countless influences during our kendo journey. We learn many things from many different teachers. These must be reflected upon as they shape who you become. We filter the good things, and maintain a steady course in the right direction with check stops along the way.

Second, since we are not professionals; the time spent doing kendo must be shared with work and family. This is not easy overseas. Especially in cities like Hong Kong where everyone is so busy, we need good time management skills to do *keiko*. You also need support from family, friends, and even your company. I guess the key is having good relationships, otherwise it can affect your practice. I would add that the quality of *keiko* is extremely important. Each *keiko*, if at all possible, should be done consciously moving forward in the right direction.

Third, I have taken the 8-dan exam several times, but this was the first time I could do it in a healthy condition. The first time, I had an Achilles tendon problem preventing me from moving properly, the second time a neck problem which moved to my shoulder and affected my mobility. I also had bronchitis. After the first fight last year, I already felt that my breathing was weakening. Simply, you need to be in an excellent psychical condition.

This time, in preparation for the exam I prioritised my health by warming up correctly, stretching after practice, and doing other exercises. I also decreased my drinking.

For me, these were the basic things that I did in preparation. Furthermore, I constantly searched for the next level in kendo. This time in the 8-dan test, I not only felt the technical level of the test was important, but also the mental side. Speaking of technique, at the test I saw many kendoka whom I have met at international tournaments, people who were part of the Japanese national team, or people who I read about in magazines. They are all strong kendoka, but in the end they could not pass.

After the exam, I really thought about that. What was different between passing and failing? In the end, I came to the conclusion that it's not just technique. The mental side is equally if not more important, especially *ki*. You must focus on how you can perform to the best of your capabilities and make yourself stand out in front of the judges. If you only demonstrate technique, you will not be able to move the judges – you must show something more. Trying to search for what this "more" is in *keiko* is very important.

NAGY: Is that something "more" an individual trait? Can it be different for each person, or is it just a calibre issue?

KISHIKAWA-SENSEI: It is probably both. First, you need to know what you are good at. Like an artist, you should know what your style is. Kendo in the end is called an art, so the sensei watching your exam are looking for your "art", or what you are good at. What exactly is it that will convey to others that this person is in fact an 8-dan? You need to have something special, personal or different about your kendo so you stand out.

NAGY: If we were to think about this in terms of *shu-ha-ri* (守破離), you are then talking about the *ri* part aren't you?

KISHIKAWA-SENSEI: If you are trying to understand this in terms of *shu-ha-ri*, first the *shu-ha* (mastery of basic training) must be already done. For *ri*, you have to demonstrate that you completely understand and have mastered all the basics. In other words, you have digested and mastered all that you have learned to this point, and that you have entered a different stage. *Ri* refers to having something special, and this is what the examiners want to see. In my understanding, the *shu-ha* is what everyone must do to meet the most basic of criteria for the 8-dan test. *Ri* on the other hand is much more individual. I think that it is *ri*, that something special above and beyond *shu-ha*, that the judges are looking for.

NAGY: What was the place of the Nippon Kendo Kata in your preparation?

KISHIKAWA-SENSEI: It was very important, especially in a place like Hong Kong where we don't have many high-level opponents. Through *kata*, we can improve the mental side of our kendo.

NAGY: We did the Nippon Kendo Kata for a documentary program a few weeks ago. It was the first time that we did *kata* together, and I was quite nervous.

KISHIKAWA-SENSEI: Exactly. Through *kata* training you must match your mind with your opponent's mind. To synchronise with the opponent is very difficult even though the movement is fixed. In this sense, *kata*, and the process of learning to synchronise yourself with your opponent, was very important for the mental training I engaged in for my test.

NAGY: As a Brazilian, what did you bring to the test that was different?

KISHIKAWA-SENSEI: In fact, I don't think of myself as a Brazilian. I know that my background is very different from the Japanese who were trying the exam that day. I was born and raised in Brazil, I represented Brazil in many competitions, but I now live in Hong Kong. I would say that I am more of a global citizen than any particular nationality. I am a representative of overseas kendoka, not just Brazilians. I think that my background being different from the Japanese who were trying the exam that day in fact helped me to think differently as to what should be done in my kendo training and development. My overseas status allowed me to stay away from the homogenisation that happens in Japan owing to its culture, which therefore allowed me to choose, develop, or stick to my own direction.

NAGY: Looking at the response on Facebook and other social media, many foreign kendoka were inspired by your achievement. What about on the Japanese side? How do you think the Japanese kendo community views your pass? What effects will it have?

KISHIKAWA-SENSEI: Many sensei congratulated me, which

reflects their expectation of the further internationalisation of kendo. Most of the sensei had a similar view that the door was open for higher *dan* practitioners from around the world to take the 8-dan test. Probably the community in Japan is going to be stimulated by more and more overseas kendoka trying for higher *dan* grades, and I believe that they will develop a good relationship through exchanging culture and technique, both of which will be useful for the development of kendo.

NAGY: What direction do you see kendo going? This means your kendo, and kendo globally.

KISHIKAWA-SENSEI: As I mentioned, I don't know what the next step is, but I know I need to search for what 8-dan should be.

NAGY: What did you feel the moment you read your number on the promotion board? What did you think?

KISHIKAWA-SENSEI: When I saw my number, the first thing I thought about was my family. My father, my mother who always supported me, my wife; without them, I would not have gone to Japan in the first place. The first thing that came to mind was now I could go home and express my gratitude and appreciation to my family for all their support and sacrifices during this long and difficult journey. Of course, I also thought about all my teachers. In fact, I doubted many times if I could really achieve this goal. These sensei encouraged me, telling me I should keep trying as I have potential. This really helped me continue, and I really want to thank them. These are the things I thought about when I saw my number; feelings of immense gratitude and appreciation, not "I finally did it, great!"

My wife asked me afterwards when I came back if I was happy. I told her that I felt relieved in that a big commitment was fulfilled. It was a very different feeling to "happy". I don't know what words can really convey the feeling I had, but I suppose it was a sense of accomplishment and achievement, andgratitude for the support I received from so many around me.

NAGY: As we were driving to the interview, you mentioned that you have climbed one mountain and you don't yet see another mountain to climb. You said you need to find another mountain to climb for the next step in your kendo development.

KISHIKAWA-SENSEI: Yes. For my own kendo development, I believe I have many things yet to do. Achieving 8-dan was the first step to go to the next level. I am eager to explore and discover the next stage of my kendo.

NAGY: I remember that Mochida Moriji-sensei said that when he was 50 and 60 he could still depend on his physical strength but as he grew older, when his legs, hips and strength gave way, he had to focus on the mental side of kendo.

KISHIKAWA-SENSEI: It's so true. In fact, I really felt that in this exam. When doing the *tachiai* with four Japanese, especially in the second round, I felt everyone was really strong in the mental side of kendo. In this round, it is no longer about the physical side, it is almost entirely mental, and you can really feel it. But the good thing about this is the training style that we have done up to now really works, and I was fully prepared to do what was needed.

NAGY: When we train together, you make sure that we do lots of *kihon*.

KISHIKAWA-SENSEI: Yes, my *keiko* is *kihon*. I am not flexible enough to change between *keiko* style, *kihon* style and *shiai* style of kendo. So for me, the kind of *keiko* I do in the dojo is the same kind of kendo I do in *shiai*. I think this is the right way. If you keep changing your kendo in different situations, you are left wondering what your real kendo is. Of course, when we practice with children or lower *dan* grades etc., you need to adjust, but the *keiko* itself is basically the same. As you know, that is what we do in practise, and to be honest, it is not much different from what I did in the exam.

I have no intention of changing the way we in terms of its frequency or intensity. Changing practice for an exam is not good as it is only a small part of kendo, and not its purpose or goal. What you are always doing, if it is correct, will naturally get the results you are interested in achieving.

NAGY: What was your state of mind after the exam?

KISHIKAWA-SENSEI: During the day of the exam, my tension was the highest it has been in my kendo life because I had already passed the first stage once. The first stage requires so much energy, and you must be mindful to ensure that your level does not drop. Instead, you must do the opposite; increase your mental focus and your spirit for the second stage. The conundrum is that there is a long time between the first and second stages. The first stage takes place in the morning, and the second stage takes place at 17:00–18:00 the same day. You must have the mental stamina to maintain and enhance your focus throughout the day. In

November in Tokyo, it's cold, and the building is even colder. You must use your mental energy to fight through the cold and your nervousness to rise to the last stage of the exam. That night I could not sleep. Not because I was not tired, but because of the tension and stress from the day still lingered deep inside my mind and body. The first time I felt I could rest was Thursday night [the day before this interview]. Today, I am starting to feel relaxed, so perhaps the interview was good timing today, as yesterday I was still very tense.

NAGY: What are the expectations for you as the new 8-dan in Hong Kong?

KISHIKAWA-SENSEI: Without a doubt the expectations of me will be higher in Hong Kong, in Brazil, and among all the sensei and kendoka, too. I think expectations among the Japanese teachers will be very high as well. As I mentioned to you, my achievement has opened up the opportunity for many 7-dan sensei to challenge for 8-dan. I also sense that teachers in Japan have some hope for me in the workings of the kendo community. I think I am ready for this. In fact, I have many people supporting me.

NAGY: I am sure that you have many things to think about and share.

KISHIKAWA-SENSEI: I have to review now and see what would be good to pass on to my fellow kendoka. This exam gave me, like all exams and tournaments give us, something to contemplate and learn from. I could learn many things from passing the exam , but it is still early days and I need time to reflect on what I have learned, how to assimilate that knowledge, and how to convey it on to the next generation of kendoka.

NAGY: Do you have any final words?

KISHIKAWA-SENSEI: We practise kendo in the spirit of "*kōkenchiai*" (交剣知愛—Mutual respect through crossing swords). Many people from around the world contacted me through Facebook and other social media, through phone calls and other means of communication. Those people that I fought in competitions from long ago contacted me to congratulate me. It really brought alive that meaning of *kōkenchiai*. I really want to thank all those around the world who supported me on this long journey. I would also like to say that I know it is very difficult to practise kendo, and not all places are easy to train in, but don't get discouraged. Don't give up, keep trying to improve

your kendo. We can always find a way to get better. For me, kendo is a way to improve as a person. We just need to focus on practice, correct practice. Once again thank you to everyone for your support. I hope everyone will continue to challenge the higher levels.

NAGY: On behalf of *Kendo World* and as your student, I would again like to congratulate you on your inspiring achievement and willingness to share that experience. I am sure that your example has already energised the training of many overseas to follow your example.

KISHIKAWA-SENSEI: Thank you. *Kore kara mo, yoroshiku onegai shimasu*!

The 61st All Japan Kendo Championships

By Michael Ishimatsu-Prime

The 61st AJKC will be remembered for two things: Tokyo's diminutive Uchimura Ryōichi winning his third title, and the emergence of Hokkaido's young Andō Shō.

By defeating Chiba's Kotani Akinori with two *kote* strikes, Uchimura claimed his third title and became only the fourth kenshi to win three or more championships. In doing so, he joins the illustrious list of Chiba Masashi (1966, 1969, 1972), Nishikawa Kiyonori (1987, 1989, 1994) and Miyazaki Masahiro (1990, 1991, 1993, 1996, 1998, 1999). At only 33 years of age, Uchimura still has a few more years at the very top, so it is possible that he could add to that tally. Miyazaki Masahiro was 36 when he won his sixth and final championships, but still competed in another two before he retired.

In his eight appearances in the AJKC to date, Uchimura has won it three times (2006, 2009, 2013), been runner-up three times (2005, 2010, 2012), and once finished third (2011). The only other kenshi who had more experience than him in the AJKC this year were Saitama's Yoneya Yuichi (tenth entry) and Higashinaga Yukihiro (ninth entry), and between them they have managed a third-place (2008) and runner-up (2011) respectively. Uchimura's closest rival has probably been Kanagawa policeman Takanabe Susumu, but as it looks like he has retired, he is clearly out on his own now.

Uchimura is well known for his lightning-fast *kote* strike—something which I am lucky enough to have been on the receiving end of during *keiko* a couple of years ago—but his *men* strikes in this AJKC were also fast and strong. Perhaps the pick of the bunch was the audacious *men-kaeshi-men* that he scored against Andō in the semi-final. K8-dan Shigematsu-sensei, Kendo World commentator at the AJKC, said it was a marvellous strike and that he had never seen anything like it before, especially at a competition of this level. He also commented that Uchimura is at such a level now, he can strike from anywhere at any time. Furthermore, even though his opponents know he will probably strike *kote*, he does so with such conviction there is nothing they can do to stop it.

Uchimura left the *shiai-jō* after each of his matches avoiding all eye contact. Between bouts, he could also be seen standing facing the wall, not looking at or talking to anyone. It is likely that he was engaged in some kind of mental training to get into his IPS (ideal performance state).[1] Whatever he was doing to prepare himself worked, because in each of his matches he appeared to be "in the zone" from the moment the *shimpan* called "*hajime*". I have heard Uchimura being described as "*nebari-zuyoi*" (tenacious), and he certainly was this year. Of the 63 matches in the AJKC, in only 13 did competitors score two *ippon*. Four of those 13 were victories by Uchimura. Only his first and third round matches went into *enchō*.

But this AJKC was not just about Uchimura's

continued rise, it was also about the emergence of Andō Shō. At the age of 23, he was already making his second appearance; his first was last year as the Hokkaido representative when he was a fourth-year student at the mighty Kokushikan University. With Kokushikan, he won the prestigious student's team and individual championships, and in his first AJKC he lost in the second-round to eventual third-place finisher, Amishiro Tadakatsu of Hyogo. Andō competed in the AJKC with the type of maturity that belied his age. In the quarter-final match he fought Furukawa from Kanagawa, a hugely experienced kendoka with police team and WKC victories to his name. However, Furukawa struggled to deal with Andō's *seme* and was eventually beaten by a *men* strike in *enchō*.

In the semi-final Andō met Uchimura and gave a good account of himself, but was ultimately undone by a *kote* and the aforementioned *men-kaeshi-men* in just 4m22s (matches from the quarter-finals onwards are 10 minutes). Uchimura showed him that his time is not just yet. However, he will certainly be one to watch in the future, and great things are obviously expected of him as he is now training with the Japanese national team in preparation for the WKC in 2015. Both competitors left the floor to a rousing round of applause from the spectators at the Nippon Budokan.

Apart from Uchimura and Andō, there were some other great performances. Runner-up and Japanese national team member Kotani was great throughout the day, as was Shōdai Masahiro (Tokyo) and Katsumi Yōsuke (Kanagawa) who met in the quarter-final in their first appearance at the AJKC. Shōdai's victory demonstrated the importance of *tame*—not striking or reacting to the opponent needlessly, but remaining mentally and physically composed, ready to strike at the right moment. Osaka's Furukawa Kosuke had been solid throughout the competition, but was ultimately undone by Andō in the quarter-final. Shiga's Mikumo Yūsuke was making his debut at the age of 24. He graduated from Meiji University last year and now works for one of the powerhouses of company kendo, Toray Industries. The famous *nitō* kendoka, H8-dan Toda Tadao-sensei, was a Toray worker when he won the AJKC in 1962 and 1964. Mikumo has a good pedigree, winning the Inter-High high school team competition and finishing third in the national student team competition, and has also won the Todōfuken tournament (Prefectural) and finished second in the National Sports Meet. In one of the big upsets of the day, Mikumo beat the 2011 runner-up Higashinaga Yukihiro in the first round with a *kote* strike in *enchō*. He then met the giant *jōdan* kendoka, Oguma Kenji from Hiroshima, in the second round. He lost in the third round to Chiba's Kanari Kaoru. He will no doubt be back again.

I am sure that Uchimura will also be back next year, and if he wins again, he will move into clear second place on the list of most AJKC victories. Whether he does or does not, one thing for sure is that *Kendo World* will be there keeping you updated on the day's proceedings.

Endnotes

1 For more information on IPS, see Blake Bennett's "The Kendo Coach" series in the KW issues 4.4-5.4.

HANSHI SAYS

A series in which some of Japan's top Hanshi teachers give hints of what they are looking for in grading examinations based on wisdom accumulated through decades of training.

NAKANO MAKOTO (HANSHI 8-DAN)

Translated by Alex Bennett—*Kendo World* would like to thank Nakano-sensei and *Kendo Jidai* Magazine for permission to translate and publish this article.

"Put your body and soul in your shinai as you strike with a vigorous spirit…"

Nakano Makoto was born in Ibaraki prefecture in 1927. After graduating from the Nemoto Youth School, he entered the Katori Navy Air Service, and saw out the end of the war in the Suzuka Navy Air Service. He entered the Keishichō (Tokyo Police) in 1949, becoming a kendo instructor there in 1958. He retired from the police in 1988. He has served as kendo instructor for the Nippon Budokan Budo School and as an official for various kendo organisations. Nakano-sensei passed the 8-dan examination in 1979, and was awarded Hanshi in 1989.

"Show enough spirit to make the examiners lean forward in their seats…"

The root of kendo lies in mortal combat—kill your enemy or be cut down. There is a saying, "*kenkon itteki*", which means "all or nothing", or throwing yourself completely into a task. This kind of mentality is important in a promotion examination. There are five points that I take particular notice of when sitting on a grading panel:

1. Does the candidate have appropriate *chakusō* (tidy appearance) and etiquette for a *kōdansha* (high ranked practitioner)?
2. Does the candidate have a strong, clear voice coming from the gut?
3. Does the candidate have an indomitable spirit and posture, an air of grace, and a dignified style of kendo based on its correct principles (*riai*)?
4. Is the candidate's *chūdan* stance resplendent?
5. Are the candidate's techniques executed with a coalescence of mind, *waza*, and body in accordance with the principles of the sword?

I expect each candidate to demonstrate these qualities during their *tachiai* at gradings. It must always be remembered that examinations are opportunities for kendoka to assess their own kendo, and ensure they are practising in accordance with the concept of kendo, which is "to discipline the human character through the application of the principles of the *katana* (sword)." Think about this concept in the course of your everyday training. Recently, I have noticed a disappointing trend in which candidates seem to have forgotten this basic premise, and lack preparedness.

I would like to see more candidates take the initiative and attack their opponent strongly with "*sen*". You must make the examiners lean forward in their seats. If you can do this, a strike that is only 80 per cent will look 100 per cent.

At the Keishichō, Masuda Sadanosuke-sensei taught us the following:

1. Man fights to win the battle of survival.
2. In kendo, too, you must strive to beat your opponent. But, there are conditions. You must abide by the rules and not

have evil designs.
3. Throwing yourself into attack is the superior method (mentally and physically).
4. In the case of *aiuchi* (simultaneous striking), *men* wins against *dō*. Even if the *dō* strike is faster and the *men* is late, this is *aiuchi*.
5. Always look to attack. Apply pressure (*seme*) and strike as your opponent steps back, or if they move in. You will find freedom through applying *seme*, and lose it if you retreat.
6. There is a teaching in the Yagyū school of swordsmanship, "Victory is half a step forwards". In other words, "*sen*" is the secret and you must always try to take the initiative and attack first. Offence is the best defence.

I passed the 8-dan examination on my third attempt (when I was 52). I did all that I could to make sure that the examiners kept their eye on me by showing my determination to win, and training hard to be able to put my all into each attack.

"If the opportunity is not there, don't strike…"

If your heart is set on winning or striking, your opponent will be able to see various openings in your mind, *kamae*, and movements. So, when you face an opponent, be of the mind that there is no enemy or self, be brimming with energy and single-minded resolve, pressurise your opponent from the *issoku-ittō* interval, and strike in one swift movement with *shin-ki-ryoku-itchi* (unification of mind, power and technique). Amply lift the *shinai* overhead, and bring it down strongly. Energise yourself and carefully observe your opponent's movements. As soon as you sense an opening, act on it without delay by throwing yourself into the attack.

Never lose heart during the strike through fear that your opponent will stop or counter you. Never be afraid of your opponents. Pressurise them with your *ki*, create an opening in their defences, and then make your strike with total commitment. This is the secret for success in kendo, but you have to train each day with the intention of learning the right time to throw yourself into the attack. It is vital that you put your body and soul in your *shinai* as you strike with a vigorous spirit.

Morishima Tateo-sensei once said at a *keiko-kai*, "If the opportunity is not there, don't strike!" He also said, "*Seme* with *ki*, but strike with *ri* (logic), and use the *shinai* with the feeling that it is cutting rather than hitting the target."

Recently, there are many people who do not hold the *shinai* correctly. The little finger of the left hand should wrap around the bottom of the *tsuka* without any part protruding. If you are guilty of this, then you will never pass no matter how often you strike your opponent. I also think it is important that you can take advantage of the five striking opportunities: "*debana*" (just as the opponent is about to strike); when you have blocked their attack; when their attack is finished; when the opponent is retreating; when they have come to a standstill.

Kendo would not be possible without a partner, so you should show respect to them, and have the stamina and fortitude to keep fighting right to the end. It does not matter wherever or whomever you are training with or competing against, have this attitude all the time.

"Assail the opponent's centreline and strike…"

As I am quite short at 165cm, I try to make my *kamae* as big as possible. In order to achieve this, I use my left leg. Ogawa Chūtarō-sensei once said, "The hollow at the back of the knee will stretch if you extend your fibula (calf bone). This will also stabilize your hips and make your stance solid. This will in turn eliminate tension in the shoulders. This is correct *shizentai* (natural standing position)." The lower body should be unyielding, and the upper body relaxed.

I also trained relentlessly in *kirikaeshi* and *uchikomi* until I understood my optimum *maai*. This really formed the platform for my kendo, so I am glad that I did it. *Kirikaeshi* is a comprehensive exercise. You learn how to hold the *shinai* correctly, control the power usage of your hands (*tenouchi*) to make crisp strikes (*sae*), footwork, *maai*, respiration, and so on. These are the most fundamental aspects of kendo.

In the Keishichō's kendo manual, *kirikaeshi* is explained in the following way: "All four limbs should be flexible, the palms sensitive, and the movements sharp. Physical and mental strength coalesce, and as the strikes are executed with *ki-ken-tai-itchi* (unification of spirit, sword and body), the practitioner also learns the correct distance to strike (*maai*). Practitioners should be taught to strike in big, correct and swift movements. If their strikes are imperfect, allow them to hit your *men* so that they learn proper technique." Reconsider the importance of *kirikaeshi*. Start making each strike in a big, correct, and slow movement. Then move on to big, strong, fast, and relaxed. This is something that kendo practitioners of all levels can and should work hard at. It is no exaggeration to say that the quickest way to improve in kendo is through practising *kirikaeshi*.

In summary, put your heart and soul in the *shinai*, and attack abiding by the principles of kendo with a full spirit, correct posture, grace (*kigurai*) and *ki-ken-tai-itchi* as you pressurise your opponent's centre. This is what I look for as an examiner. Approach your regular *keiko* with the intention of being able to express the toils of your training at the next examination.

GRADING SUCCESSFULLY: Part 1

By Shigematsu Kimiaki, Kendo Kyoshi 8-dan
Translated by Remi Yamaguchi

Those who train in kendo regard grading examinations and matches as a means for cultivating self-discipline. Passing a difficult grading exam is especially motivating compared to regular training. However, it is also a tremendous disappointment when you fail. There are those who have been able to pass each grading examination without failing once, and others who become stuck on a certain level. So what is the difference between these two groups? If you can figure this out, even just a little, you are one step closer to being successful.

In a grading there are many things for you to tackle, including how to impress the judges by striking your opponent in such a way that it leaves an impression. There is no way to achieve your goal without accomplishing this. What I will write about in this article is based on things I learned from the guidance from my sensei, what I actually felt through my own experiences, and what I read in books and instruction materials. I hope you will find this information useful in achieving your goals.

"Strike your opponent in a way that you will leave an impression on the judges…"

1. Why you need to take a grading examination

The "Concept of Kendo" determines that kendo should "discipline the human character through the application of the principles of the *katana* (sword)", and the purpose is to nurture kendo practitioners with high standards.

In the "Concept of Kendo", nothing is mentioned regarding "promotion to a higher rank" or "winning matches". If somebody asks you why you want to take a grading exam, how do you answer? Many people do not have a clear answer for this. I do not either, but perhaps mine would be something like this: "To have my skills as well as my understanding of the spiritual elements which underlie kendo that I have learned over many years of training, evaluated in detail, so that I know what to focus on next."

Kendo training consists of constant repetition. You cannot acquire the skills overnight, but by continuing to train honestly and with conviction, I believe that your efforts will bear fruit.

2. Gradings: It's not about the actual strike, it's about the *seme-ai*

I think a grading is where you get to express your kendo philosophy. What exactly is a "kendo philosophy"? It is the kind of mental attitude you have while training, or how you acknowledge kendo and practise it. Furthermore, it is whether or not you are training according to the "Concept of Kendo". One of the ways of testing the effectiveness of your *keiko* is to engage in matches, but it becomes a matter of whether you are result-oriented, or if you keep the "Concept of Kendo" in mind at all times, and train yourself while being aware that kendo is a traditional martial art for self-development.

As your examination day approaches, your mental attitude at training becomes the main focus, and you are expected to demonstrate your approach. Your kendo philosophy changes depending on your mindset, but it is important to cultivate a healthy attitude and resolve through everyday training.

I will consider the examination itself from here. You might think it is a matter of competing against your opponent on the number or quality of effective strikes scored. Effective strikes are important, but mental elements (such as spirit and your *seme*) are equally important as evaluation criteria. The higher the grade, the more you are expected to show that your strikes are intentional, otherwise you will not receive a good evaluation. You need to keep in mind that just because you can strike your opponent does not mean that you can pass. At gradings for high-ranking kendoka, strikes should represent your desire to mentally beat your opponent. Therefore, gradings are not a striking competition, but are about *seme*.

If you complain, "I didn't pass even though I struck my opponent", it is only a sign that your outlook on kendo is immature and underdeveloped.

3. Who do you fight against at a grading?

Your opponents are roughly the same age and rank; in other words, people of the same skill level. Judges will evaluate your overall performance including your attire, *reihō*, posture, *maai*, *seme*, striking opportunities, *zanshin*, and so forth in the limited time given. Examinees need to demonstrate their techniques and the mental elements acquired through training in a short amount of time.

Examinees are divided into groups of four. All the examinees need to do two *tachiai*, and it is important that you stand out. Furthermore, your performance needs to stand out more than anybody from the previous groups. When I say "stand out", skills are a given, but the higher up your rank is, the more your spirit needs to be conspicuous. If your performance is just ordinary, you will have a long way to go before you can pass.

4. Are you properly clothed and do you demonstrate proper *reihō*?

Many judges pay attention to your attire, as you are not judged solely on whether you struck your opponent or not. Untidy attire is likely to be considered a reflection of your mind.

When wearing a *hakama*, it does not look good if the front is lower than the back, or if the back is lower than the front, or if the *kendō-gi* is puffed-out at the back. These things do not have any direct effect on your kendo performance, but you look very sloppy when you are not clothed properly. High-ranked practitioners are required to have an adequate air of dignity and grace.

What reflects dignity and grace the most is your posture. Prepare carefully, because without the proper attire, you do not even qualify to sit the grading.

In the grading, you will need to show what stage of discipline and training you are at. Your behaviour and manners need to exude elegance and confidence. This cannot be superficial. The examiners will look closely at you to see whether your manners are a pretence, or are a part of you as a result of your daily training. The examiners will not be fooled by temporary acts of propriety.

Those who are training regularly will be able to carry out the series of movements smoother, from taking the *taitō* position (*shinai* placed on the left hip) to *sonkyo*. Nothing forced about it, and you should be able to synchronise your movements with those of your opponent. Manners show your attitude towards kendo and are requisite for high-ranking practitioners are required to have. Your attire and manners reflect your mental attitude in everyday life. I hope all of you will pay attention to this in your daily practice.

5. *Sonkyo* required for an effective strike

Perhaps many people think that *sonkyo* is just a simple act of squatting down and standing up afterwards. It is necessary to recognise the fact that the quality of *sonkyo* determines whether you will have good *seme* and be able to produce a valid strike.

People say that *sonkyo* requires a posture and a

mindset like that of a lion. This means that when you do *sonkyo*, your spirit needs to be replete like a lion which has found its prey and is ready to pounce. You need to have a sturdy back and legs to be able to do good *sonkyo*. Then you will be able to concentrate *ki* in your abdomen. If you do not, your *sonkyo* may not be as good, which means you will have a hard time focusing *ki* in your gut.

The most important thing is to have your weight on your knees, keep tension in your lower abdomen when squatting down, and maintain it until you stand up. In reality, many people relax too much and stand up carelessly. They want to attack their opponent, but it is too late. Not many people realise that once you relax your attention at the time of *sonkyo*, your opponent will be one step ahead of you, and already have an advantage.

When I attended a nationwide workshop, the instructor said, "*Sonkyo* should be just like smoke rising from incense." This means that when doing *sonkyo*, your neck, back and waist need to be extended and straight just like incense smoke rising towards the sky, and your movements must be smooth and not falter.

You need to be careful when doing *sonkyo*, especially when you get a chance to train with your instructors. Basically, you will not go wrong if you adhere to the Nippon Kendo Kata. If you follow the lead of the *motodachi* (*uchidachi*), when you are *kakarite* (*shidachi*) you will be able to have a good *keiko* with *ai-ki* (*ki* synchronised with your opponent).

6. Elements of *datotsu*

Kamae, *seme*, striking opportunity and *waza* selection, strikes, and *zanshin* are made as one complete movement, which is then evaluated as a *yūkō-datotsu* (a valid strike).

(1) Kamae

The word *kamae* means "To have the proper stance and attitude for the purpose of being able to react to any situation." *Kamae* influences your striking movements, so through repeated *keiko* it is necessary to develop proper *kamae*. It is often said that the "*kamae* is alive", meaning "a *kamae* that enables strikes at any time", or "a *kamae* that allows instantaneous movement"; in other words, a *kamae* from which you can react immediately.

Kamae consists of two parts: *mi-gamae* (body) and *ki-gamae* (mind/spirit). If you are standing so that the body is aligned in a straight line, the upper half and the lower half of the body will synchronise properly and be stable. As you stand up from *sonkyo*, take care so that your *kamae* looks big. You can do this by relaxing your shoulders, sticking out and opening your chest, and standing so that your ears are over your shoulders. The easiest way to open up your chest is to pull your shoulder blades a little closer. For the arms, there is a teaching that you should position them as if you were cradling a baby. You should be able to move the *shinai* freely as long as your chest is sufficiently open.

In *kamae*, the position of the left fist is important. Place it approximately one fist's width away from the body so the joint at the base of the left thumb is facing the navel. Some people are tall, short, thin or heavyset. Keeping the basics in mind, figure out a *kamae* that best suits your physique with the left hand set and the body stable so that it easy to swing the *shinai* up with the left hand.

People look uncomfortable at gradings because they are worried about their *kamae* so much that the upper body is tense. Superficial postures can be compared to artificial flowers. They may look pretty at a glance, but if you take a closer look at them, you realise that they are not real. What is the difference? It's the "fragrance" —artificial flowers do not have it. You should do your best to come up with a *kamae* so that your intense spirit and grace can be perceived.

Pay attention to the eyes as they greatly influence your *kamae*. If you look as if you are staring down from the top of a small hill with a straight back and relaxed shoulders, you will not only be able to move swiftly, you will also put pressure on your opponent.

(2) Hassei (Vocalisation)

One of the characteristics of kendo is the constant shouting. There are two kinds: calling out the designation of the target area you are striking, and *kakegoe* (making a sound to encourage yourself and pressure your opponent). Vocalisation also increases your concentration. In other words, by intentionally vocalising, you encourage yourself, and gradually increase your concentration through uplifting your spirit, which then enhances your state of mind. The kind of *hassei* that reveals full-spiritedness is the real kind of *hassei*. I believe it turns into some kind of invisible power which can be felt by your opponent.

For *kakegoe*, for self-encouragement, it is best if you try to exhale from your lower abdomen in a deep, crisp voice. Making the proper sound is one of the important techniques of kendo. Pay attention to your *hassei* when training. *Hassei* is directly related to your posture. Your *hassei* will be substantial if you stand using the muscles in your lower abdomen with your shoulders relaxed. If your posture is incorrect, you will not be able to store energy in the lower abdomen, which results in a muffled *hassei*, and you will be unable to intimidate your opponent. Surprisingly, many people think it is acceptable to *hassei* at any time, while in reality there are distinct *maai* from which you can and cannot. *Hassei* must be done at a safe *maai*. This is because right after shouting you will have to inhale, and when you do so, you become temporarily "empty" and volatile. Therefore, if you *hassei* when you are at *issoku-ittō-no-maai*, you risk being struck when you inhale afterwards.

The reason why you vocalise when you strike your opponent is so you can concentrate your power in the attack, not only at the time of impact on the *datotsu-bui*, but afterwards as well. You express your hidden determination instantaneously in the form of a strike, and by vocalising simultaneously, your power and strength become complete.

There is a teaching that says *hassei* is "*aun-no-kokyū*", which means matching your breathing with the opponent's. For example, if you intend to strike your opponent's *men*, "*a*" is when you start with "*me*", and "*un*" is when you conclude it with "*n*". Not only is it important to articulate both sounds, but you also need to keep each sound short and raise the pitch at the end. By doing so, your abdomen tightens, and your left foot gets pulled up faster. You need to utter a sharp sound, and at the same time, your voice needs to reverberate and linger in the air like the resonating sound after ringing a bell. Try not to lose the momentum of your strike.

(3) From tōma to shokujin (blades touching); from shokujin to kojin (blades crossing) and issoku-itto-no-ma

• **Closing the *maai***

There is the maxim, "You are close to your opponent, but your opponent is far from you." Of course, physically this is not actually possible. So why is this expression used in kendo instruction? It actually refers to mental distance, teaching you to always maintain a psychological superiority over your opponent. It is important to pressure your opponent and instantaneously strike the target when an opening arises.

Both start the *seme-ai* (pressure each other) from *kamae* at *tōma*. The *maai* shrinks to *shokujin*, then *kojin*, and then *issoku-ittō-no-ma*, and the tension

increases. While the *maai* is closing, you enter the *uchima*—the distance from which a strike can be made.

In many cases, examinees just stand with their feet immobile. Maybe they are too focused on their *kamae* to worry about their feet, but they seem to be just standing. If you just stand and shout "*yaa, yaa!*" you will not be able to intimidate your opponent. Once you stand up from the start line, you need to close in on your opponent. It is quite critical whether or not you have strong enough *ki* to make your opponent retreat, enabling you to step deep into their territory. When doing so, it is important that you do not waver. Even though you know that you need to be close to your opponent in order to strike, at the same time you experience feelings that distract you such as "I don't want to be struck". This clouds your mind and makes you hesitate. Being close to your opponent means you are more likely to get struck. However, you have no choice but to overcome your fear, be resolute and step closer to your opponent with strong energy, ready to face them. This movement pressurises and intimidates the opponent.

•**Seme**

Since long ago, there have been sayings like, "Do not strike and win; win and strike", or "The one who wins the battle of *seme* has the right to strike". These tell us about the importance of *seme*. Even today we hear expressions such as "Pay more attention before striking," or "Work hard before striking". These sayings teach us that *seme* is more important than striking. Basic concepts in kendo are "*seme* with *ki*, strike with reason" and "win with *ki*; strike with reason". So why do you need to *seme* your opponent? This is because you need to create an opportunity to strike. "Win with *ki*" and "*seme* with *ki*" are to make an opportunity to strike. These are basic principles of kendo.

In other words, you need to make efforts to find and create opportunities to strike, or lure your opponent to do so. This effort is called "*seme*". To *seme* does not only mean using the tip of the sword, but also the whole body and the feet. All together this becomes *seme*, and when your opponent feels psychological pressure and becomes agitated, that is a sign that your *seme* is actually having an effect.

In many cases, however, while you may be trying to *seme* your opponent, in reality it may not be effective. You need to create in your opponent a sense of fear in your opponent that you are going to strike them. This will make them disconcerted. The ability to *seme* cannot be mastered overnight. The judges will not miss this subtle change in the examinees' minds, and they will carefully watch to see who is winning the battle of *seme* and dominating the other. They then use this information to decide who passes or fails.

What is wonderful about kendo is that elder sensei can beat younger, faster kendoka. This becomes possible by not relying on speed, but rather by incorporating various elements into kendo, step by step. These elements are "experience" and "*kiryoku*" (mental power). You may lose your physical strength as you get older, but your *kiryoku* becomes stronger through many years of training. Eventually, your *seme* will start showing through the tip of your *shinai*, which will compensate for your lack of speed. Strong *seme* only becomes possible when various factors are combined, and it is a reflection of your strength in kendo.

The following phrase by Saimura Gorō-sensei, a Hanshi 10-dan known as a "sword saint", demonstrates the importance of *seme*: "No matter how quick your *waza* is, it is created in your mind. If you are able to control your mind, by extension you should be able to control your *waza*." This remark shows how *waza* is connected to *seme*, and is something we need to keep in mind and strive towards for as long as we continue to train in kendo.

• **Controlling the centre**
In order to be able to *seme* effectively, you must first control the centre. One of the main methods to do this is through manipulation of the *shinai*. To score a *yūkō-datotsu* (valid strike), the movement of the tip of your *shinai* is crucial. Without moving the tip of the *shinai* (*kensen*) from the centreline, *seme* from above or below, *omote* or *ura*, and take control of the centre in response to the opponent's movements. If you can remain psychologically poised and *seme* your opponent without moving from the centre, your kendo will appear to be, and will be very strong.

There are several ways to take the centre such as using *hari-waza* (slapping the *shinai*), *osae-waza* (suppress) and *maki-waza* (wind) and moving the body. There are also variations of *kamae* such as high or low, or with a rigid or soft grip. It is important to know which *kamae* to use depending on the situation.

Is it okay as long as the *kensen* is kept on the centreline? Your mind should be in the centre as well. Your left hand reflects your mind: if your left hand is shaky, naturally the tip of the *shinai* will move away from the centre. Saimura Gorō-sensei said, "When your left hand moves, you have lost even if you are not struck." Therefore, controlling the centre with the left hand is of the essence.

Many practitioners misunderstand the strength of the *kensen*. If you truly have strength in the *kensen*, it means that you have flexibility. For example, even if your opponent tries to push your *shinai* down from the *omote* side, you can return the tip of the sword back to the centre without forcibly pushing back. Also, if your opponent tries to execute a meaninglessly *waza*, in order to let them know that it was not the right moment, you can thrust the tip of the *shinai* towards their throat in response. This is what being flexible means. On the other hand, rigid people have an unyielding grip and *kamae* that cannot respond sufficiently.

Often there are people who, when their opponent tries to strike *men*, do *mukae-tsuki* to control their strike. Kenshi who do not flinch in the face of their opponent's strike deserve great credit. However, it makes me wonder if it is good to do so regardless of the situation. It shows that you are unable to seize the openings in your opponent's movements. Being able to do *mukae-tsuki* to control an opponent's strike is important, but it is also important to react in a flexible manner and countering with *debana-waza*, *suriage-waza* or *kaeshi-waza*. If you only do *mukae-tsuki* in reaction to your opponent's attack, you are effectively saying that you are not flexible enough to do any other *waza*. The expression "If you only do *tsuki*, your *waza* will cease", warns people to not do that, so please keep that in mind. (This is a play on words. "*Tsuki*" from the verb *tsukiru* also means to "exhaust" or "be finished".)

• **Maintaining your own rhythm**
As you close in on your opponent little by little, you will experience mental tension. Strive to "maintain your own rhythm". It is vital that you maintain your own rhythm and disrupt your opponent's. In other words, even if you synchronise your breathing with your opponent, you should not match your *ki*, and vice versa. Try to break your opponent's rhythm while maintaining your own, and get them to fight according to your dictation.

As you face your opponent, your distance gets closer little by little, and your desire to make a strike becomes stronger. At this stage you are still even with your opponent. The key to success is to break the deadlock and get into a mental state that works to your advantage. As you get closer, you start trying to subtly provoke each other. If you are too desperate to strike, you will lose your composure and only focus on your opponent's movements. That is to say, if you are not mentally composed, you will not be able to determine whether the openings in your opponent's *kamae* or movements are real, or if they are intentional openings designed as ruses to lure you in. In this case, you will end up making a careless strike. This can result in being struck with *debana-waza* or *ōji-waza*. In this type of situation, the judges will probably think that your opponent is in control of the bout.

Determine whether the openings you can see are a result of your *seme*, or were created intentionally. You need to understand that there is a significant difference between a strike that occurs in a situation when you pressure your opponent so much that they were forced to act, and one that was made when your opponent was composed and acts freely.

In *Gorin no Sho*, Miyamoto Musashi wrote that there are two kinds of seeing: "*ken*" and "*kan*". He said that *ken* is weak and *kan* is strong. *Ken* only sees the surface, but *kan* looks deeper and sees the opponent's mind. When your opponent intentionally creates an opening, be patient and maintain your own *kamae*. That way you will be able to maintain your rhythm. After you patiently disregard your opponent's trap, if you take a few steps forward he or she will not be able to wait any longer, which will disrupt their rhythm. If that happens, they will desperately try to regain their beat, and in some cases, they will try to carelessly strike you instead. Take advantage of that opportunity and counter with *debana-waza* or *ōji-waza*. This will certainly impress the judges. Conversely, if you try to force your opponent to act but they do not respond, this will confuse your own timing, so you need to be careful. This type of mental battle is important and the examiners acknowledge it at gradings for the high *dan* ranks. Understand that patience is critical at gradings.

(4) Striking opportunities and *waza* selection

- **Creating opportunities for strikes by initiating attacks**

Often I hear people say, "You won't pass a grading if you do not strike *men*", or "You shouldn't strike *dō* at gradings". Certainly *men* might be the basis of kendo *waza*, but the *datotsu-bui* are *men*, *kote*, *dō* and *tsuki*, so you should not focus solely on *men*. Be flexible, seize the opportunity and strike. Easy at it sounds, it is something that everybody struggles with. I read soemwhere, "Listen carefully and you will hear a sound. However, even if you clear your mind you will still not be able to hear your opponent's thoughts. It's the same with bells. You can keep hoping for it to ring, but hoping is not enough. You need to actually ring it physically to make the sound. To make your opponent's heart sing, **you need to move it first**. Keep this in mind when training." My interpretation of this is that you have to be proactive to create striking chances.

Many examinees do not seem to know what *seme* is. They have good *kamae* and energy, but their problem is that they do not take the initiative enough. I often see matches where examinees stand up from *sonkyo*, wait until they are full of energy, and then try to strike. Or, some are so keen to initiate attacks that they try to strike as soon as they see their opponent move. Sometimes both examinees keep trying to cut each other with the same *waza*. Or, they think they need to strike *men* first and then *kote*. Unfortunately, when I see such matches I do not feel their energy at all.

Keep in mind that if you think you should wait until you stand up after *sonkyo* to focus your *ki*, it is already too late. You need to make your spirit replete when you are bowing to your opponent. That way, after you stand up from *sonkyo* and assume your *kamae*, you have already taken the initiative.

In high-level kendo, whether or not you are able to take the initiative is the determining factor in who the winner will be. Nobody can remain calm when an opponent steps in to their *maai* full of energy, and there will be a moment when they instinctively react. This is the purpose for initiating attacks, and iit s when opportunities for strikes are created. You will need to train hard to achieve this.

When you try to strike your opponent, when you try to defend, or when you are confused and freeze, the state of your mind is reflected in your actions. It is important to look for these in your opponent and select the correct *waza* to use. Good opportunities will arise only when you initiate with *seme*. Waiting will not create good opportunities—create them yourself.

- ***Waza* lies ahead of *seme***

Waza can be categorised into two groups: *shikake-waza* and *ōji-waza*. *Shikake-waza* requires you to not miss the moment and strike instantaneously when your opponent has reacted to your *seme*. *Ōji-waza* requires you to execute a *waza* in response to your opponent's strikes.

Be careful when you are executing *ōji-waza* to first *seme* your opponent to take the initiative and apply pressure. Whilst applying pressure, give your opponent the impression that they have room to attack so that they make a strike. That is when you should strike. Why do people end up striking when they are under pressure? This is because the situation is not in their favour, they feel desperate to turn things around and regain control, and come to the conclusion that striking is the only solution. As a result, attacks are initiated without proper mental preparation.

(5) Strikes

Landing a valid strike during a grading is an important element that determines if you pass or fail. However, you are required to not just strike the *datotsu-bui*; the strikes need to have reason, too. Your strikes must conform to the proscribed basics, be full of energy, and your movements before and after must be good enough to "touch the judges' hearts". You will not be able to move anybody unless you pour all of your energy into the strike.

What decides whether your strikes in a grading or match are considered valid or not is an extremely significant issue. Let us take *men* as an example. The instant your *shinai* makes contact with your opponent's *men*, this is merely a hit and not yet valid. It is only considered a valid strike (*yūkō-datotsu*) when the entire process is completed. In this case, to complete your strike means to remain full of energy until the end of the striking movement, and to maintain your posture. The cut itself is more important than anything, but whether you can complete your strike or not is the deciding factor in its validity.

An *ippon* is an absolute necessity in a grading, but will not count if they land accidentally. It is therefore important to take the necessary steps to make an intentional valid strike. The most effective way to do *keiko* is to be fully aware of the importance of taking the *shodachi* (the first strike) in all of your bouts. In other words, by always being determined to make the first strike and completing it.

Another vital aspect is to build up *tame* (tension) when you strike. Sometimes you are told, "Your strikes don't have *tame*", or "You must strike with a little more *tame*". So what is *tame*? It is a little difficult to explain, but my understanding is that you need to wait for the moment when your opponent is startled and starts to move. You then seize the start of that movement. If you are too eager to strike, you are likely to execute *waza* before your opponent moves. However, if you wait too long, you will freeze and will not be able to take advantage of good opportunities to execute *waza*. *Tame* can be understood to lie between excessive eagerness and being settled, and the only way to be able to strike with *tame* is through constant *keiko*.

In a grading, strikes that are not strong or sharp enough are unlikely to be regarded highly. People tend to think that strikes depend only on the control of your *shinai*; but while the hands that hold the *shinai* can generate sharp cuts, the movement of the feet is equally important. The right foot is the "*seme* foot", and the left is the "power foot". When you strike, push off with the left foot and stamp forward with the right, and then pull your left foot up immediately. The harder you push off with your left foot, the more resounding the stamp with the right foot will be.

(6) At a grading your spirit must overwhelm your opponent—a requirement to pass

Overwhelm your opponent with your energy and spirit, and then execute *waza*. You only have a very short time during grading exams to show your stuff, and you need to have the mindset that it is a real duel with swords, i.e. if you lose, you lose your life; strikes must be made with *sutemi*, absolute conviction. The spirit that burns like fire and intimidates the opponent will decide the outcome.

After a grading, some candidates who did not pass may not comprehend why and say, "Even though I hit my opponent, I still didn't pass." Let me again summarise the criteria for scoring a *yūkō-datotsu*. You need to have a replete spirit, correct posture, and show *zanshin*. Spirit must be the foundation of your *waza*, and when this is missing, you may hit the target but it will never be a *yūkō-datotsu*.

I would like to write about some incidents that demonstrate spirit. The first was at the Chiba Prefecture Embu Championship in April, 2008. In this competition I thought my *men* and *kote* strikes were good, and my sensei who observed the match said so, too. However, Hanshi 8-dan Iwadate Saburo-sensei said that I did not have proper energy. Back then, I did not understand why he made such a remark. After that, I had the chance to receive instruction from him several times, and each time he told me that I lacked energy. Right before my 8-dan grading, Iwadate-sensei told me to fully display my fighting spirit. I was able to pass 8-dan at that grading.

Another time, I participated in an Examinee's Seminar held in Tokyo. I learned how important it is to face your opponent with a high level of spirit. I was told, "If the level of the opponent's energy is 100, yours should be 120. If the opponent's level of energy is 120, then yours should be 150." The lesson here is that your energy should always exceed that of your opponent.

The origin of kendo is in sword fights to the death. If you were facing an enemy in a situation like this, you would fight and try to win with all your might. Promotion examinations are no different. Once you stand up, you need to show greater spirit than your opponent. Your spirit must be felt by your opponent, and resound with the judges at the same time. You must show that your determination to win is stronger than any other examinee.

In kendo, those with a strong spirit show it in their eyes—they are full of life. On the contrary, those with low spirit have eyes that look weak. Overwhelm your opponent with your spirit, and when openings occur in their mind, *kamae* or actions, strike at that opportunity with absolute conviction. That should result in a *yūkō-datotsu*. Even if it is not judged as a *yūkō-datotsu*, it will still have value.

Those who overwhelm their opponent with their spirit and strike with absolute conviction stand out. One second they strike their opponent, and the next they have already passed through. Their footwork is smooth, which enables them to strike, do *zanshin*, and charge at their opponent in one seamless movement. A high level of energy is the lifeblood of kendo.

(7) Examiners pay special attention to patience after a *yūkō-datotsu*

Judges always pay attention to how a match proceeds after a *yūkō-datotsu* has been scored. If you are able to execute a *yūkō-datotsu* first, that will give you a mental advantage; but if one is scored against you, this could make you hurry. This demonstrates how important it is to score the first *yūkō-datotsu*. One of the criteria that examiners are required to pay attention to is the winning rate. Let us assume that you could score a *yūkō-datotsu*. How you fight after this determines whether you pass or fail. I understand that you want to get another, but if you try to strike your opponent and end up getting struck as a result, your former *ippon* will be considered moot. You need to keep this in mind at all costs.

One of the secret teachings of the Yagyū-ryū school of swordsmanship is, "Following the lead of your opponent is the key to victory." What I think this means is, according to the *maai*, you must try and make your opponent strike you. Therefore, patience is vital after completing a strike. If the match ends as it is, it means that your opponent will lose because of your *ippon*, so he will become agitated and impatient as the desire to get a point back increases. Even if your opponent tries to strike you, be patient and quickly suppress them without allowing them to strike. If you can respond to your opponent exactly in the way described in Miyamoto Musashi's teaching *"makura no osae"* (nipping the enemy's technique in the bud), this will make him frantic. Desperation makes you unstable, and openings manifest in strikes that are made in this frame of mind. This presents a good opportunity to strike *men*, *kote* or *dō*, and execute various *waza* taking advantage of the circumstances. If you can do this, you will be able to rise above the rest of the examinees. It is this difference in defence and attack that stands out, and is what examiners look for. Consequently, this is the difference between those examinees that pass, and those that do not.

(8) How to concentrate at a grading exam venue

After you arrive at the grading venue, whether or not you are able to maintain your concentration until the end of the exam, I think, is a big part of the result. I assume all the examinees go through a rigorous training regime to prepare even though it is challenging for most people to secure enough time for training with work and family commitments. Taking exams is also a financial burden because of transportation and fees, etc. Every time you fail, you need to pay more. That is all the more reason why you have to pass.

You arrive at the venue, feeling determined to pass. So far, so good. The problem is that you are likely to meet peers and acquaintances once you are there. You enjoy the reunion and a nice chat. Even though you have been training so hard, and trying to maintain your concentration, you lose your concentration, and in many cases fail because of it. From my experience, even though you might think it rude, try to refrain from talking to others. It is that important to not lose your focus. After passing the first stage of the 8-dan grading exam, I stayed in the top seat at the venue and did not talk to anybody before the second stage. To be honest you cannot help but feel nervous, but ignore your anxiety. Overcome your nervousness and passing the exam becomes more realistic.

(9) Keiko after grading is very important

Everybody trains hard in preparation for grading exams, and those who pass will practise even harder. Contrarily, those who do not get the result they wanted may actually lose motivation. Some may even take a break from training for a while. I can only imagine how disappointing it must be to have your dreams shattered, but the important thing is to continue training. If you stop *keiko* because you failed a grading, it is like the whole purpose of your training was to pass the exam and nothing else. You can never hope to pass with the level of your determination to succeed being so low. You need to start preparing yourself for the next exam. Should you fail and experience disappointment, train even harder with more determination.

Another thing I would like to point out is that you never complain about the result. Often, many who do not pass will say things like, "My opponent did strange kendo", which is just an excuse. Chances are they are saying exactly the same thing to their friends about your kendo. Making this kind of comment is the same as blaming your opponent for your loss, which means you are unaware of the lack of your own ability.

Those who pass, on the other hand, sometimes say, "I was lucky I had a good opponent". Making this kind of remark is the same as claiming that you were successful only because your opponent was accommodating, and it was just sheer good fortune. It is almost as if you do not deserve to have attained your rank. Kendo requires you to work with others, and it is not acceptable if you win or lose because of your opponent's skill level. Train yourself very hard so that it is irrelevant who you come up against.

THE NUTS 'N' BOLTS OF KENDO

By Nakano Yasoji, (Kendo Hanshi 9-dan)   Translated by Alex Bennett

WAZA TRAINING

How should a teacher structure technical training?
Compared to the old days, kendo now is predominantly focused on competition. Success in matches is a major objective, especially for younger practitioners, so it is important to coach them in various techniques for this purpose. When I was younger, competition kendo was not so much of a consideration, and we trained mainly to get strong in body and mind.

Times change, but before teaching students various techniques which can be useful in *shiai*, it is vital that they are able to perform the basics properly. This means correct posture, gaze, footwork, *kamae*, and all of the essential components in *kihon* that are a prerequisite for technical advancement. *Waza* training also requires considerable repetition. I recall an instructor at one university who was very skilled at *kote-men*. In fact, that is pretty much all he taught. This kind of training is valid to an extent, but in kendo it will not do just to be good at one technique and deficient at others. For this reason, students should be taught various techniques from the outset.

In terms of what sort of *waza* to teach, it depends on the level of the students. If they are advanced, then there are countless variations and high level technical principles and combinations that can be taught. However, with lower level students it is effective to teach them the "ins and outs" of techniques such as *harai-waza* first. The opponent's *shinai* can be parried in different directions such as from the *ura* and *omote* sides, from above, and from underneath. Another standard technique is to attack the opponent's *kote* and then strike *men*. Or, attack *kote* and lift the *kensen* to pressurise the throat, and just as the opponent lifts their hands, an opening for *dō* will be revealed (*kote-dō*). In this technique, do not strike *dō* immediately after *kote*, but pause and pressure the throat first, then strike *dō*. This is the kind of detailed advice that an instructor can give to motivate students.

Or, strike *men*, and if the opponent blocks it, immediately revert to *dō* (*men-dō*). Or, strike *men*, and as the opponent eludes it, follow up immediately with another *men* strike (*men-men*), or a *tsuki* (*men-tsuki*). Attack the opponent's *tsuki* and strike *men* when he steps back, or *kote* if he tries to move in. *Tsuki* followed by *kote* was a favourite technique of Mochida Moriji-sensei. Two-step techniques are effective, and should be practised over and over.

Then there is *debana-waza*. Just as your opponent is about to move, strike their *men* (*debana-men*). Or, strike their *kote* as they launch an attack. There is also *debana-tsuki*, but this is not taught very much anymore as it is hard to score if the opponent is moving forward.

For *tsubazeriai*, when you push your opponent's hands, they will push back, so you can use this opportunity to step back and strike *men* or *kote*. If the opponent senses that you are going to strike *men* and lifts their hands up to block, then revert to a *dō* strike. There are many possibilities, but for all *shikake-waza* techniques it is important to teach students to react depending on each situation rather than just striking randomly. That is, to strike at the right opportunities.

For techniques countering the opponent's attack (*ōji-waza*), *suriage-waza* is excellent. When the opponent attacks, deflect the *shinai* and make a counterattack to *men* or *kote*, or *gyaku-dō*. Actually, *men-suriage-gyaku-dō* is not so common, and it is more appropriate to strike *kaeshi-dō*. There is also the possibility of *nuki-dō*. If the opponent attempts a *kote* strike, dodge it and counter with *kote-nuki-men*. If the opponent attacks *men*, it is effective to move slightly out to the side with *hiraki-ashi* and strike *men*.

So, my point is to teach students thoroughly in the most popular techniques first, and then gradually delve into the high level of more sophisticated *waza*. Avoid devoting the majority of *keiko* time to arduous exercises such as *uchikaeshi*, and be sure to include ample opportunity to enjoy learning various *waza*.

What I have been talking about so far is regular technique training. Once the form of the *waza* has been learned to a certain extent, the next step is to put it into practical use. An instructor should make openings for the techniques to be employed at first. Gradually make it harder so that the student has to think about how to execute the techniques against an opponent who is not cooperative. You can then use this opportunity to explain the intricacies of using the *kensen* to probe the opponent's defences. Fix

their bad habits as they learn, and finally when they have a grasp of these ideas, they will then be able to apply the techniques in a bout.

There are so many waza in kendo to learn. It is only natural for people to want to focus on the techniques that they are good at. How important is it to practise all of the waza in kendo?

You have to try as many things as you can when you are young. If you just work on one thing, or a limited number of techniques, your kendo will not expand. Everybody has their speciality. If you are good at striking *kote*, then work hard at it so that you become famous for that technique. But, also remember that potential opponents will look for ways to defeat you based on your proclivity to use that technique, so having more up your sleeve is the only way you will be able to prevail.

In the old days, kendo teachers didn't explain techniques in much detail. They would just say "You will work it out on your own". What do you think of this attitude?

Kendo practitioners in the old days were confident in their ability, so they were rarely taught verbally. Even Takano Sasaburō-sensei never lined students up and lectured them. Sugawara Tōru-sensei and Satō Ukichi-sensei also of the Tokyo Higher Normal School where I studied never tried to express techniques in words. They would answer questions if we had any, but otherwise they just let us get on with it. They believed that lecturing in techniques was not the way to learn. Times are different now though.

In a way, it is like learning Japanese calligraphy. All it takes is to teach the basic form, and then leave the student to work out the rest. If he does not study he will not learn, but he will quickly get fed up if you keep overloading his head with information. Practitioners do kendo because they like it, and they like to think about it. So, I prefer just to give students pointers if they are making mistakes.

What is the best way to make the most of gokaku-geiko?
Gokaku-geiko is sparring between practitioners of equal ability, but there is almost always disparity in the level of skill. Never engage in sparring with the attitude that you are much stronger than the opponent. Instead, you should always have a sense of humility. Also, when sparring against your sensei, have the attitude of wanting to take a point off him. Have the determination to try and score, and at the end of the sparring session, say thank you, do *uchikaeshi* to finish up, and then move on to your next partner. If you are an instructor, and your student wants to keep going, it is okay to let him get one last point in, and humbly concede by saying "*Maitta!*" (you win) to give him confidence.

Takano Sasaburō-sensei is said to have been very good at bringing the best out of his students while sparring in hikitate-geiko.
I was able to train with Takano-sensei. He fought from *chūdan*, and he would easily pick *kote* off. Then he would tell us to take *jōdan* against him. It felt rude taking such an aggressive stance against a great sensei, but he insisted telling us that it would make our spirits stronger. He wanted us to take that same aggressive spirit and apply it to our *chūdan*. After making a good strike from *jōdan*, he would acknowledge it, we would do *kirikaeshi*, and then finish.

How should you tackle tricky kendoka?
When I go to train at Kōdansha's Noma Dojo, there are some very tricky individuals indeed. I wonder what will become of kendo when I fight them because of their unorthodox style, but really it is a matter of learning how to deal with all types. It is all about rhythm. Often a tricky player will not come when you think he will, and will attack when you think he won't. I remember fighting somebody recently, and just as I thought he was coming in to strike *men*, he went for my *dō* instead. It really threw me, I must admit. If an opponent has an unorthodox or awkward style, go with the flow and match them tit for tat with your own style. It is a good opportunity to learn.

How should shiai-geiko (match practice) be done?
When students do match practice, it is best to have referees deciding the points. It is the same for older practitioners, too, as it adds to the tension. With or without, it is important that practitioners keep in mind the right distance, *kamae* and so on, and try to learn from *shiai*. It is not beneficial if students are fighting the same opponents all of the time. It is very important to have variation, and to fight people they are not used to. Then they can really test themselves, and have plenty to think about when they are successful, or when they get hit. It is really important to get used to the unfamiliar.

REI
DAN
JI
CHI

The Greater Meaning of Kendo

Reidan-jichi Part 16

KIHON-DŌSA: No. 5

By Prof. Ōya Minoru (Kendo Kyōshi 7-dan)
International Budo University

Translated by Alex Bennett
Some sections of the text incorporate previous translations of Ōya-sensei's work by Steven Harwood

Kihon-dōsa, or basic movements, refers to *kamae*, footwork and the manipulation of the *shinai*. In other words, it entails all of the principles behind striking and thrusting movements for scoring *yūkō-datotsu* (valid attacks) in kendo. In the last issue of *Kendo World*, I looked at the biomechanics of the striking process. In this issue, I will look at the four basic techniques in detail.

1. Men (*shōmen*, *sayū-men*)

Simply put, the process of striking *men* entails stepping forward with the right foot while lifting the *shinai* overhead, then bringing the *shinai* down to strike. *Sayū-men* is the same, but the *shinai* is brought down on an angle of 45° from the left or the right when striking.

Main points for consideration:

Footwork and *shinai* manipulation must be executed cohesively. The overhead and downward swing and strike to the target should be made in one smooth movement. Throughout the striking process, the left and right hands and the *kensen* should not veer away from the body's centre. In the case of *sayū-men*, the correct blade angle for the strike should be made by turning the hands above the head and while swinging down; but care should be taken to keep the left hand in line with the centreline of the body. If the right hand is over-utilised in lifting the *shinai* overhead, the resulting strike will be too right-handed, meaning that the body will become unbalanced and the strike will be made only with the hands (instead of the whole body) with an incorrect trajectory.

Start the strike with the left hand. Also, make sure that you do not just stick your arms out and strike with the upper body leaving your lower body behind. At the point of contact, the left hand should be at solar-plexus height, and *tenouchi* (grip) should be tightened upon impact. The back (left) foot should not fly up at the back, but should be snapped up quickly behind the right foot by sliding it swiftly along the floor. Relax the tension in your upper body immediately after impact so that the *kensen* rises (bounces) naturally about 10cm above the *men*. If upper body power is not relaxed, the strike will appear forced, and you will be unable to make the transition into the next action easily as your *shinai* will be pressing down on the opponent. After the strike is made, continue shuffling through with the feeling that you are piercing the opponent with your left hand, and make each step incrementally smaller.

2. Kote

Stepping forward with the right foot, the *shinai* is lifted up far enough so that the opponent's right *kote* is visible from under the hands, and then is brought down for the strike.

Main points for consideration:
First of all, be sure not to look at the *kote* when striking. In principle, the *kote* strike should be made from above the opponent's *shinai*, rather than below it. As the lift-up for the *shinai* is smaller than that in a *men* strike, the lack of power generated overhead should be compensated for with a strong stamp of the right foot, and a firm tightening of the grip upon impact. If the left foot lags behind after making the strike, you will come to a stop at an interval that is easy for the opponent to counterattack, and you will be unable to follow up and switch to the next action because of inadequate posture.

Be sure to snap the rear foot up quickly as the strike is made, as if you are trying to slide in and ride over the opponent's hands. Also, relax the tension in the upper body as soon as the target is struck. This will enable the *kensen* to rise naturally from the *kote* strike to the height of the chest. Move in close to the opponent after the strike using the momentum generated by the swift movement of the left foot. This will enable you to remain alert and ready for any counterattack.

3. Dō

While stepping out with the right foot, the *shinai* is swung overhead, the hands are turned and the strike is made on the downward swing. Right-*dō* (your left) is considered to be the standard target, whereas left-*dō* is referred to as *gyaku* (reverse). Striking left-*dō* is permissible depending on the situation and opening, but is generally only awarded in special circumstances. *Dō* techniques are usually executed in reaction to the opponent's movement rather than as a self-initiated strike.

Main points for consideration:
Be sure not to focus your gaze on the opponent's *dō*. The upper body must be flexible, and the wrists should be particularly supple. Both the left and right arms should be extended when the strike is being executed. The strike should not be made only with the right hand, nor should the *shinai* hit the target from below. If your hips (lower back) are not driving the strike, your posture will become unbalanced, and it will be difficult to follow up quickly with another technique if necessary. The left hand should not stray from the body's centerline, and it should be positioned in front of the lower abdomen. Be sure to tighten the grip instantaneously on impact.

After the strike, it is possible to shuffle through on the right side or the left. Given the theory behind cutting the torso, it is better to follow through across the body to the right hand side so that your left side skims past the opponent's left shoulder without spinning around too much to the right. As you shuffle through, reduce the tautness in the wrists, and move the left fist up the *tsuka* to touch the right.

4. Tsuki

In the case of the two-handed *morote-tsuki*, step forward from the right foot while twisting both hands inwards in a squeezing motion and extend the arms to complete the thrust to the throat. With one-handed *katate-tsuki*, step forward with the right foot while releasing the right hand attaching it to the right hip, and use the left hand to direct the *shinai* into the throat while twisting the wrist inwards.

Main points for consideration:
Be sure to make the thrust from a square-on position in front of the opponent. Thrust with the hips and hands together, not just by extending the arms. The left hand should not lift up or veer from the centreline. When attempting the one-handed *katate-tsuki*, quickly attach the right hand to the right hip as the thrust is made in order to maintain balance. In either case, immediately return to *chūdan* after the thrust is made. In other words, do not continue pushing through with the thrust, but pull the *kensen* back as soon as it touches the target.

5. Taiatari (Body clash)

Taiatari is the act of following through and colliding with the opponent after attempting a technique, and using your momentum to knock the opponent off balance and force another opening to take advantage of. *Taiatari* must be executed in combination with a technique, otherwise it is an unlawful act and will be penalised. Follow up with a strike as soon as the opponent is unbalanced by the force of the clash.

Main points for consideration:
Make contact with power generated from the hips, not the hands. It is important that the left foot is snapped up as the *taiatari* is made to add power to the forward movement from the hips. Do not look down on contact, and make sure both hands are situated in the front lower abdomen region as the hips plough in for the clash. If the opponent is knocked back, chase them and strike forwards. If the opponent remains in the same position, it is effective to bounce off to the left or right and strike while going backwards (*hiki-waza*).

In receiving *taiatari*, use *suri-ashi* to slide the right foot forward as the opponent crashes into your body, while keeping your hands down and power concentrated in the lower abdomen. Snap your left foot forward as soon as contact is made to firm your lower body and hips. Try and hold your ground without lifting your hands up. If your left heel is flat on the floor when receiving, you will be knocked off balance, so keep it raised to absorb the incoming shock. Judge the power and timing of the opponent's *taiatari*, and as you receive it by sliding your right foot forward, bring your left foot up to counter the incoming force with your hips.

6. Tsubazeriai (Tussle)

Tsubazeriai is the tense tussle at close quarters with the *tsuba* locked together. The distance is even closer than the *chika-ma* interval. Your *shinai* should be held vertically and slightly to the right, the elbows lightly extended, and the hands down in front of the lower abdomen with both *tsuba* locked in place. Both look for opportunities to attack with *hiki-waza*.

Main points for consideration:
As the positioning in *tsubazeriai* is so close, it is dangerous for both sides. You must never let your guard down, and constantly look for openings to strike. The *tsuba* must be locked together at lower abdomen height. Never place your *shinai* on the opponent's shoulder, or bring the *shinai* around to the inside position as this will be penalised. Also, make sure that your posture is upright.

In the next instalment of "Reidan-jichi", I will analyse the finer points of *kirikaeshi*.

"Mumyō wo kiru"
(Sever ignorance)

When the warrior thinks only of the way in which he should hold his sword, he becomes preoccupied with matters of form and fails to see what is transpiring in front of him, thereby reacting inappropriately. He looks, but he cannot see. This is "mumyō", or ignorance.

Kawasaki Ginosuke (?–?)
Lived around the beginning of the Tokugawa period (1603–1868) and started the Tōgun-ryū, but little else is known about him.

Famous members of the 47-Ronin, such as Ōishi Kuranosuke, were students of the Tōgun-ryū. This school of swordsmanship was founded by Kawasaki Ginosuke. Little is known about this particular warrior except for the fact that he was a fervent student of swordsmanship since childhood. He may have come from the province of Echizen, but this cannot be verified. It is said that he prayed to the deity of Mt. Hakuunzan and was enlightened to the secrets of swordsmanship, which he systemized and decided to call "Tōgun-ryū". He possibly studied under a sword master named Tōgumbō which is why he chose to name his school Tōgun-ryū using the same *kanji* characters. Again, the truth is shrouded in mystery, but some speculate that this was in fact the priest Tōgun Sōjō of Mt. Tendai. Or, maybe he was taught by a Hieizan priest known as Myōgi Hōshi, who could actually have been a legendary *tengū* goblin-like creature called Myōgibō who lived on the mountain. Alas, everything we know about this man is speculation.

He was not keen to share his divine knowledge with people outside of his direct family line. It was his great-grandson, Kawasaki Jirō Taifu, who really made a name for himself demonstrating the same brilliance in *slice-and-dice-jutsu*. He set forth on his *musha-shugyō* adventure, travelling through the provinces in search of worthy opponents to duel. He killed a swordsman in Kumagaya, and the dead man's students wanted revenge. Jirō Taifu fled the little

SWORDS OF WISDOM

By
ALEX BENNETT
Based on the book
"KENSHI NO MEIGON" (1998)
by the late Tobe Shinjūrō
Used with author's permission.

village with a throng of would-be avengers in pursuit. He was forced to fight his way to freedom, and was successful to a point, but wounded and outnumbered, he was eventually overwhelmed. Poor Jirō Taifu was dragged before the magistrate in Edo, but the judge pardoned him of any wrongdoing, and actually commended him on his remarkable feats with the sword.

He was subsequently employed in various domains to teach swordsmanship, lived to a grand old age as he continued refining his technique, and amassed many students of considerable influence. In fact, from the Tōgun-ryū style sprang 24 branch schools, and a further 60 or so subsidiaries of these, and it was taught in over 20 feudal domains throughout the country.

The philosophical basis of this school lies in the teaching "mumyō wo kiru". Mumyō is originally a buddhist term which refers to a state of "ignorance" or "darkness". It is "Avidyā" or, "a misunderstanding of the nature of reality; more specifically–a misunderstanding or misperception of the nature of the self and of phenomena." So to "sever" the ignorance away is to remove all uncertainty. Darkness blinds the swordsman. "A swordsman in the darkness can't see the trajectory of the enemy's sword or guage the spatial interval. He is frightened of the flash of the blade, averting his eyes and holding his breath, wincing when surprised by the enemy's shouts. Panic stricken, he will lunge in for the attack, but will end up short and probably cut his own foot off."

The real nature of human beings is weak and easily befuddled, which can easily lead to your own demise. How can this be overcome in swordsmanship? According to the wisdom of the Tōgun-ryū, lower your stance, straighten your back, take three steps towards your enemy, and on the third step forget your enemy, forget your self, and attack with *mushin*, or no-mind. As you move in, your sword gets shorter. Your 3-*shaku* (91cm) blade becomes 1-*shaku* (30cm), then 5-*sun* (15cm)… If you can do this, you will be able to achieve the "particle technique" or "*mijin-no-kurai*".

Even though 9-*sun* (24cm) or 5-*sun* (15cm) are considered very short lengths in terms of weaponry, it still cannot be hidden. If a sword is as tiny as a particle, it can be concealed on any part of the body, as if it is your body that is the blade. Making your sword like a particle of your body is part of the process for reaching the ultimate state of "no-sword" or "*mutō*". This is what the great swordsmen aspired to, but ignorance or *mumyō* prevents transcendence to this realm of perfection of mind, body, and technique. The darkness must be severed before you can be enlightened to the profundity of nothingness, and the secret teaching that size doesn't matter…

Bujutsu Jargon Part 5

Reference guide covering various bujutsu-related terminology

Bruce Flanagan MA (Lecturer - Nanzan University)

 # 32 流 ryū

Schools of martial arts, performing arts and fine arts often have the character *ryū* in their title, which literally means 'flow/current/spread'. If we liken the core principles of an art to a flow of water, then the main river or style is the *ryūgi* (流儀) and the streams that branch off from the main river are *ryūha* (流派). The term *ryūha*, or just simply *ryū*, is added to names of styles, schools, factions, traditions, ideologies, philosophies, and traditions. A *ryū* usually wishes to differentiate itself from other groups and is often structured around a founder, central figurehead, or head teacher known as a *sōke* (宗家).

Yagyū Hyōgonosuke of the Yagyū Shinkage-ryū formulated the concept *sanma-no-kurai*, which means 'three stages of learning' (often written as 三磨の位). The stages are *narai* (study), *keiko* (practice) and *kufū* (alteration) and these are depicted as three points on the circumference of a wheel-like diagram in order to demonstrate the cyclical nature of learning. A student is advised to (1) observe and theoretically study a technique, (2) master the technique through actual practice, and then (3) experiment with and change the technique. For further improvements the process is repeated. Other learning concepts are illustrated in the maxims *shu-ha-ri* (守破離) and *shin-gyō-sō* (真行草).

 # 33 三摩之位 sanma-no-kurai

 # 34 スポチャン spochan

Spochan is an abbreviation of 'sports chanbara' (スポーツチャンバラ), a freestyle system of weapon-versus-weapon competition developed by Tanabe Tetsundo. Sports chanbara features bouts between competitors wearing lightweight padded helmets and wielding sponge-covered inflatable weapons such as daggers (*tantō*), short swords (*kodachi*), long swords (*chōken*), two swords (*nitō*), shields (*tate*), short staves (*jō*), long staves (*bō*), spears (*yari*) or glaives (*naginata*). The point-based sport has gained a considerable international following with the Japan Sports Chanbara Association and the International Sports Chanbara Association overseeing international tournaments.

#35 ちゃんばら chanbara

Scenes of swordplay and sword duels seen in samurai movies and historical dramas (*jidai-geki*) are typically called *chanbara*, which may be written in either hiragana or katakana. A sword-fighting movie may be called a *chanbara-eiga* (ちゃんばら映画) and a stage show or drama featuring swordplay may be called a *chanbara-geki* (ちゃんばら劇). Another name for the genre of sword-fighting movies, dramas and plays is *kengeki* (剣劇 / 剣戟). Children playing fighting games with toy swords is called *chanbara-gokko* (ちゃんばらごっこ).

#36 護身 goshin

While various budo feature self-defence in their curricula, the actual word used to refer to self-defence is *goshin*, with self-defence techniques being called *goshin-jutsu* (護身術). The word *goshin* is used in terms such as *goshin-tō* (護身刀), a sword carried for self-defence (also *mamori-gatana*). The term for acting in self-defence is *jiko-bōei* (自己防衛) and for the legal nuance of legitimate or justifiable self-defence, the term is *seitō-bōei* (正当防衛). *Goshin* should not be confused with another word *goshin* (誤審) which means an 'incorrect judgement' by a referee.

#37 ナンバ nanba

Nanba refers to an old Japanese style of body motion or *washiki-hokō* (和式歩行) believed to have been different from how people walk and run in modern times. Researchers believe that long Japanese garments such as *kimono*, which were tied at the waist with *obi* belts, caused many people not to swing their arms, lift their knees or twist their bodies too much in their daily activities. There is no agreed theory on the origin of the word *nanba* but many examples of the movements exist in *kabuki*, traditional dances and martial arts. Nowadays when walking, most people twist the trunk of their body along a central vertical axis and swing the arm forward that is opposite to the foot they have out; i.e. they swing their right arm forward when they step forward with their left leg and vice-versa. In *nanba*-style movement the right leg and right arm move forward at the same time and are immediately followed by the left leg and the left arm. To be more specific, this is an oversimplification and, rather than swinging the whole right arm forward with the right leg, only the right hip and right shoulder move forward creating a momentary *hanmi* position. The individual then moves forward by repeating the *hanmi* position with each side of the body, having eliminated lateral twisting of the trunk. The resulting walking style has been dubbed *nanba-aruki* (ナンバ歩き). Traditional foot messengers (*hikyaku*) were said to have employed a running style called *nanba-bashiri* (ナンバ走り) that is touted to have been more practical and efficient than the standard gait of a modern runner, allowing for greater endurance and further distance to be covered. It is believed that they utilised the *hanmi* motion as well as leaning forward into the direction of movement to allow gravity to propel them forwards. In recent years there has been a surge of interest in *nanba*-style movements but there are still varied interpretations of what *nanba* actually means. Many sports scientists, coaches and *kobujutsu* practitioners are attempting to accurately recreate *nanba* movements in order to improve the sporting performances of athletes and the daily lives of modern people. Research into another *nanba*-related style of movement called *namiashi* (常歩) is also gaining popularity in martial arts circles.

Bibliography

- *Bujutsu Jiten (Zusetsu)*, Osano J., Shinkigensha, 2003.
- *Dai-Nihon Butoku-kai - Budō Senmon Gakkō-shi*, Budō Senmon Gakkō Kendō Dōsōkai (ed.), Kōwa Bijutsu, 1984.
- *Kōjien (Daigohan)*, Iwanami Shoten, 2004.
- *Nichijōgo no naka no Budō Kotoba Gogen Jiten*, Katō H. & Nishimura R. (ed.), Tōkyōdō Shuppan, 1995.
- *Nihon Budō Jiten (Zusetsu)*, Sasama Y., Kashiwa-Shobō, 2003.
- *Seimei-chi toshite no Ba no Ronri: Yagyū Shinkage-ryū ni miru Kyōsō no Ri*, Shimizu H., Chūō-Kōron-Shinsha Inc., 1996.
- *Shinka suru Nanba - Jissen Namiashi Kendō (Shinpan)*, Kidera E., Mainichi Communications Inc., 2010.
- *Wa-Ei Sports Chanbara*, Tanabe T., Soubunsha Co. Ltd., 1996.

小川 忠太郎
Ogawa Chūtarō

Why Am I Alive?

By Hamish Robison

"Why am I alive?" This was the question that Ogawa Chūtarō (1901-1992) posed to himself when he was in his teens. To seek the answer, he started on the well-worn path of the Zen warrior, and left an indelible mark on modern kendo in the process. He followed in the footsteps of such luminaries as Yamaoka Tesshū, who sought personal discovery and growth through both the techniques of the sword and Zen Buddhism. He may have been one of the last of the line of great masters going back centuries to devote themselves to this type of *shugyō*.

As chief kendo instructor at Kokushikan University, and later as a kendo instructor at the Tokyo Metropolitan Police Department (Keishichō) from 1953 until 1970, the last three of which were as *shihan*, and the man responsible for the "Concept of Kendo" that guides our practice today, Ogawa Chūtarō's influence continues to loom large over modern kendo, but to his devoted disciples who carry on his legacy, his influence has not been felt as much as it should have. As more kendo greats from the pre-war generation leave us, it has become all the more important to preserve his message.

Ogawa Chūtarō was a prolific writer and speaker, leaving a legacy of talks on Zen and swordsmanship in quite an easy and understandable manner. A keen diarist, he also wrote religiously about daily events and his experiences. It was this that formed the basis for his work *Hyakkai Keiko*, or *100 Practices*, that recounted his training with Hanshi 10-dan Mochida Moriji. His son, Ogawa Akira, is fond of recounting the sparse entry on the day he was born - "Son born" - in comparison to some of the much more lengthy entries to do with his kendo trainings.

The humility of the man comes through in the above book, but also whenever you talk to people about him. This can be seen very clearly in his attitude to continual learning throughout his life. Many people ask why there are no longer any 10-dan kendo sensei in Japan, and this, it is said, can be traced back to Ogawa Chūtarō himself. A student of Mochida Moriji and other greats of his generation, in his later years he was approached about being made a 10-dan. In a customary manner, he responded that he was nowhere near Mochida's level, and he could not be so presumptuous as to accept such an honour. Once he had said this, it of course made it very difficult for anyone else to accept being awarded 10-dan. While there must have been other factors in his deprecation of the 10-dan rank, having lived in Japan for some years, this story certainly sounds plausible.

Very few of his works have been published in English, which we at *Kendo World* saw as an opportunity to further our mission of disseminating high-level knowledge to the non-Japanese-speaking kendo world. This article therefore starts a series on Ogawa Chūtarō where we will look at the two main pillars of his investigation into his initial question: swordsmanship (both kendo and *kenjutsu*), and Zen. My research into Ogawa Chūtarō has involved lots of talking with his former students and his family, and as such, I hope to give a better picture of the man himself than what can be gleaned only from his writings and spoken recordings. We have been given access to many of these recordings and many videos of him training, both in one-on-one and normal dojo training situations.

How exactly did Ogawa Chūtarō train? What was it like training with him? How were the concepts he wrote and talked about actually translated into action? These and many other questions are hard to answer, but maybe they are important to ask for those who seek the same answers to the following questions Ogawa Chūtarō posed: Why am I alive? Why am I doing kendo? And maybe one that we find ourselves asking as the world changes drastically around us: what relevance does kendo have to modern life?

Please join us as we start this series on Ogawa Chūtarō, one of the greats of modern kendo.

LOCKIE JACKSON
UNLOCKING Japan

PART 25 — Oh the Shame

Last night, I witnessed something troubling. I had been out to dinner with friends, and was walking back to Kyoto Station to take the last train home. Realising that I had a few minutes to spare, I decided to duck into a Family Mart to pick up a bottle of water for my journey.

As I exited the store I stopped, somehow suspended in both time and motion, and gazed dumbfounded at the sight before me. A man, perhaps in his early thirties, sat legs crossed on a bench on the pavement. He was smoking a cigarette, sneering. His eyes darted around the vicinity to see how many pedestrians had noticed the power that he was now wielding.

You see, at his feet, in *seiza*, with his forehead touching the pavement, was a young man in a Family Mart smock trembling. Profuse apologies, offered in honorific Japanese, cascaded continuously from his quivering lips.

The elder man appeared to be what is known as a "*chinpira*", a low-level, wannabe yakuza gangster. He was thin, garishly dressed, and sported a ridiculous haircut and shaved eyebrows. I wanted to smack him, but I didn't. I did what everyone else there that night did - I pretended not to see. I continued on my way as if nothing was going on there at all. Why the kid from the convenience store was forced to his knees by the *chinpira* is something I can only speculate about. So is what might have happened to him after I left, but I'm willing to bet it was for the smallest of infractions. Perhaps he had made an error in the change he had given the *chinpira*, or perhaps he had handed over the wrong brand of cigarettes. In any case, it wouldn't have been for much, and the *chinpira* was loving every second of this public display of intimidation and control.

As my train pulled away into the night, I slumped into a vacant seat and began to try and make sense of what I had just seen. Why didn't anyone come to his assistance? Why had I failed to get involved? What could possibly be so wrong with someone that they felt the need to publicly humiliate someone else to the extent that the *chimpira* humiliated the young clerk? How was this blatant, wilful, and brash display of sheer and utter bullying tolerated? As I clutched for answers to these questions, I gradually became aware of the true source of my frustration. I was angry with myself. I had failed to do the right thing. I had chosen the easier choice, the one that says, "It ain't worth getting involved." I felt ashamed.

And shame, to me, is one of the more peculiar of the human emotions. Especially the way it seems to work in Japanese culture. Shame, most introductory books on Japan will tell you, is one of the foundational undercurrents of Japanese society. Clichéd as it sounds, Japan is often referred to as 'the shame society'. This means it is shame, not guilt, that regulates morality. Shame has been used to explain everything from the way politicians and corporate executives apologise for scandals, to attitudes about divorce, or homosexuality. "In our country", a Japanese colleague once advised me, "it's only wrong if you get caught". While I don't really agree with my colleague's admittedly tongue-in-cheek theory—I don't think Japanese people are any more or any less moral than people from anywhere else—I would agree that one's public persona, how one is seen in public, seems to be of particular importance here.

And so I got to thinking: how do we, as long-term foreign residents of Japan, come to grips with how to behave here? How do we decide which of the cultural values we were socialised to cherish to retain, and which of the cultural values to let go of? To what extent does our life trajectory – our living in Japan – shape us into doing things "the Japanese way"? And how comfortable do we ever truly become in this process?

I'm sometimes told by Japanese people that I'm "just like a Japanese person". I guess that these well-intended compliments are attempts to recognize that I have become, to some degree, increasingly more attune to a so-called Japanese way of doing things. But on the other hand, there are also some aspects of Japanese society that I will never quite get my head around. Perhaps that's what continues to keep Japan exciting and interesting for me. The one thing I do hope, though, is that if I ever again see a situation like the one I witnessed last night, I will be able to go and help the poor kid. I don't want to feel *that* kind of shame again.

Green Budo

By Manuela Hoflehner

When training in the martial arts, the foundation for all that we do is *rei*—respect for our partner, those who came before us, and those that we nurture to follow us. In practising budo, we take the elements of our chosen martial art and transfer them to our everyday life. The respect for our partner, sensei, sempai and kohai, in turn becomes respect for our fellow human beings and beyond, for everything that surrounds us.

This is precisely what the members of the Austrian Kendo Association had in the back of our minds when we started to organise the 2013 European Jodo Championships (EJC) in Linz, Austria. It was the first EJC that had ever been held in Austria and we were faced with several challenges. Our jodo population is quite small, none of the three people in the organising committee practised jodo, and we had little time to prepare—only a little over six months. Nevertheless, we had high standards and great expectations to make this EJC a well-organised event, and a memorable experience for all participants.

We also considered what would remain of the EJC after the event. Sporting events encourage us to become active, create opportunities for meeting new people from different cultures and spread a mutual spirit of friendship. Unfortunately, the ecological impact is often neglected, and what remains after many events is a lot of waste. With plastic bottles, disposable tableware and merchandising articles made of plastic, such events are a considerable burden on the environment. At the 2013 EJC, we strove to do it better, and had three top priorities: food, waste, and the involvement of local artists.

Regional, organic food

For the two seminar days and the competition day, we wanted to have as much organic food as possible for the catering. A talk with the chef de cuisine at our hotel made it possible. Although it was not in their regular day-to-day operation to buy organic food, they were very committed to accommodate our wishes. In the end, the catering in the hotel consisted of about 80 per cent organic food; all of it from local producers. On the competition day at the venue, a local business that specialises in organic and vegetarian catering provided 100 per cent organic food, partly even Demeter certified. Competitors were offered a buffet of three hot dishes and a salad bar.

Our most controversial decision in regard to the catering was to only offer a meat-free lunch and dinner during the event. Due to ecological and economic reasons, meat was only available for breakfast and at the sayonara party. As the cost of organic meat is quite high, it would have at least doubled the cost of lunch and dinner. In addition, excessive meat production damages the ecosystem due to the monoculture of grain and soy, and it uses up a lot of resources like water. In fact, it takes 15,000 litres of water for every kilogram of beef that is produced, and raising broiler chickens takes 3,500 litres. In comparison, wheat production uses 900 litres and potatoes 500 litres. Another

reason for us to choose meat-free dishes, particularly on the competition day, was that they are light and easily digested, making them suitable pre-competition meals. Some of the competitors were a bit taken aback by this decision—it is hard to please everybody at an event—but we tried to find a solution that would be acceptable to everybody. On the other hand, we got a lot of positive feedback from people who thanked us afterwards. The vegetarians were especially grateful, telling us that too often they had to do with side dishes, at one point even only getting potatoes with mayonnaise. However, in the end, both groups got what they wanted: at the sayonara party, we had 25 per cent meat and 75 per cent vegetarian food, and plenty of both.

Waste reduction

In the early stages of organisation, we dismissed our initial plan of providing lunch-bags on the competition day in favour of a catering service; they would have created a lot of waste. With the catering on site, waste was kept to a minimum. In addition, we had a special gift for all competitors, judges and officials. The water in Linz has been awarded "Europe's Best Drinking Water" by the European Union multiple times, and to encourage people to use tap water over bottled water, every participant received a "Retap Bottle", produced from borosilicate glass and designed and made in the EU especially for drinking water. Borosilicate glass is more eco-friendly in production and its raw materials compared to regular glass and is used in laboratories because of its high strength and heat resistance. The lid of the Retap Bottle is made of thermoplastic-elastomer, which is free of bisphenol A (BPA), so not harmful to your health. The bottle can be cleaned and refilled with tap water and reused many times.

Involvement of Local Artists

Another pillar that was important for us was to support and work together with local artists. At a seminar that had been organised by the kendo club in Biberach, Germany, we had seen how they worked together with the local *ikebana* group, who created a beautiful flower arrangement for the *kamiza* side of the dojo. Impressed by the added value and the perceptible change of atmosphere that such a small detail created, we decided to adapt this for the EJC. The local *kadō* (flower arranging) group in Linz—Sissy Födinger-Wieder and Elisabeth Höfer, who are teachers of the Ikenobo School from Kyoto, Japan—agreed to make seven small floral arrangements for the tables of the European Kendo Federation officials, as well as for those of the *shinpan-chō* and *shinpan-shunin*. This was a small detail that cost almost nothing, but added greatly to the atmosphere.

Our second, slightly bigger involvement of a local Austrian artist was for the creation of the trophies for first place. Glass artist Thomas Aschenbrenner from Linz made extraordinarily individual trophies reminiscent of drops of water or falling rain. Each trophy had three water drops (made of glass and filled with water) arranged like stones in a Zen garden.

Mobility

Another issue that we would have liked to tackle was the problem of mobility and public transport. When it comes to the mode of transportation that each nation uses to get to the venue, there is little we can do. The distances that we cross are huge in some cases, and using a train or a bus instead of a plane is an unreasonable demand. We could, however, do our best to encourage the use of public transport during the event, and also make it easier for people who were coming by train. We again imitated the brilliant service of another kendo club—our Czech friends who organise the Toru Giga Prague Cup each year. They provide the participants with detailed descriptions and maps on how to get to the accommodation and the venue. This is an invaluable help for people who are not familiar with the local public transport system and the

surroundings, and is probably the best service an organiser can provide car-less people with. What also proved to be beneficial in this case was that the hotel and the venue were only 200m apart, so all participants could actually walk from the accommodation to the championships.

Other efforts

In addition to these focal points, all helpers were given staff T-shirts made of certified organic cotton. This took some online research, but in the end we found a provider who could produce the T-shirts for the same price as conventional suppliers.

The competitors' booklets were printed at a local printing company that specialises in sustainable and ecological communication and printing, and produces cradle-to-cradle products. They are EMAS-certified and part of the "Economy for the Common Good". In the end, the booklets proved to be the highest strain on our budget, as we had initially calculated it at a much cheaper cost. The rising number of participants also had a part in this miscalculation—we had initially expected fewer competitors than the 170 visitors from 16 countries that came in the end. All in all, however, we finished the event with a balanced budget (no profit, no loss), proving to ourselves that the financial side is no limitation in deciding to hold a green event.

Room for improvement

As always, even when you accomplish a lot, there is still much that could not be done because of time or budget restrictions. There were many other ideas that we had or came up with in the course of organising the EJC that we will learn from and keep in mind for the next event. One of these was to offer a free ticket for public transportation during the days of the competition. The city of Linz would have given us a 50 per cent discount, but paying the other 50 per cent for all competitors out of our budget would not have been feasible. Similarly, we would have liked to make the glass medals for the second and third places locally, too, but ran out of time to find a supplier or an artist who could have done it. For the next event, we also learned that we should communicate more clearly and in advance what kind of food people can expect.

But, as Harald Hofer, President of the Austrian Kendo Association, put it:

"The European Jodo Championships is a rather small event. Nevertheless, 200 people can create a lot of waste. To minimise waste was one goal, easy to achieve if you are willing to think out of the box. But most important was that we wanted to show that a "green event" doesn't necessarily have to mean "limitation", but added value. Did we have a big, positive impact on the environment with this event? Maybe not a huge one—but what's more important is that I'm very sure we could change the mindset of some participants, and that's what counts. A green event is a challenge, but also very satisfying. Now that it's done for the first time we hope that there will be many copycats. The more green events, the greater the impact!"

Having an eye on the ecological part of an event like the EJC certainly takes more time, a well calculated budget, a lot of research and some creative thinking on how certain issues can be solved. On the other hand, it gave us organisers the pleasure of not having just "done the job" as asked, but going to great lengths to make the 2013 EJC special to all participants. It provided us with the opportunity to connect with more people than would have otherwise been possible or necessary (artists, cooks, politicians) and created relations with them that will remain even after the event is finished—we were linked through this joint effort for a common cause.

The 2nd World Combat Games

By Graham Sayer

In October 2013, I had the pleasure of travelling to St. Petersburg, Russia, to witness the 2nd World Combat Games (WCG). Unlike the inaugural WCG, which I was also fortunate enough to attend in Beijing in August 2010, I was determined this time to see at least one of the other sports/arts in action other than my beloved kendo.

Having some knowledge of judo, I would have liked to have seen a few rounds of that competition, but I was also curious to check out women's sumo, a version they have yet to really adopt in Japan, where I presently live.

I arrived on October 19 after a rather stressful change of planes in Moscow, checked into the hotel and went in search of fellow Kiwi, Alex Bennett. He was in the bar at the hotel, a no-brainer really.

Kendo was not due to start until October 21, so it was decided that we check out the venue the following day. Alex had some FIK duties to attend to, and unlike Beijing, there was no *Kendo World* representative in attendance, so I was asked to assist with videoing the fights.

The venue was huge and it held all the events over the eight-day competition. Kendo was to follow the sumo, and it was a little strange to see kendo advertised on the same poster as sumo. However, when I think about it, perhaps sumo has more similarities with kendo than any of the other arts represented, apart from maybe aikido.

The massive arena was divided into three areas allowing for mats, flooring, and special areas for fencing and a sumo *dohyō*.

Just like the WCG in Beijing, the events were scheduled around TV viewing times so they could be broadcast live. Each day's competitions were timed to start at around 2pm allowing for the meaty end of the *shiai* to take place during prime time. This also allowed audiences to arrive after work, which they did in good numbers for kendo.

The first day of the kendo competition got underway at 2pm on October 21. A full breakdown of results from the two days of competition can be found here: www.worldcombatgames.com/en/page/160/schedule

From my experience in Beijing, I was really looking forward to the 8-dan invitational *shiai*. When you live in Japan, you get to see 8-dan sensei competing against each other a few times a year, but add the extra nationality ingredient, and it certainly gets more competitive. The 8-dan *shiai* in St. Petersburg did not disappoint.

Some highlights of the kendo competition were as follows:

8-dan
Park Dong Chui of Korea won the first *shiai* against Funatsu Shinji by two *ippon*, which was no small feat. He went on to place 3rd overall, and I had the pleasure of presenting him with his prize. A very humble and all round nice guy!

Tagawa Yoshiteru from the USA did not place, but his fight with Furukawa Kazuo was intense and a real education; seeing Furukawa step backwards was a first. It was an excellent display of high-level kendo.

Women's Individuals.

Safiyah Fadai of Germany was by far my pick here. She took silver, losing by a *men* cut that has been well discussed in certain forums. This young lady has guts, determination and skill in spite of her relatively short kendo *shiai* career.

Men's Individuals
The Japanese did not bring the big guns to Russia due to a clash of dates with the domestic police *shiai* schedule, but their team, along with that of the Koreans, was still full of experienced kendoka. The person to shine for me was Sandor Dubi of Hungary, and his *kaeshi-dō* against Shikano Mitsunori of Japan in the semi-finals was unreal. Watch the video and check out the set up prior to the execution here: www.youtube.com/watch?v=qPaaErnqcHM

I went to Russia wondering if the WCG was where kendo really wants to be, and came away thinking "Yes, it does", and we need more countries to offer to host these combined combat games. I also enjoyed watching the Nippon Kendo Kata, the iaido, jodo, and chosunsebup demonstrations, which added to the "art vs. sport" aspect of kendo. Incidentally, I never got to see any other events, and had to settle with seeing the change in shape of the competitors in the lobby of the official hotel over the four days I was there. Maybe I'll be able to see something next time in 2016, but, does anything else really matter other than kendo?

So far, the cities vying to host the 2016 event are Da Nang (Vietnam), Melbourne (Australia), Kuala Lumpur (Malaysia), Singapore and Nay Pyi Taw (Myanmar/Burma). The decision will be made in 2014, and I'm already looking forward to going.

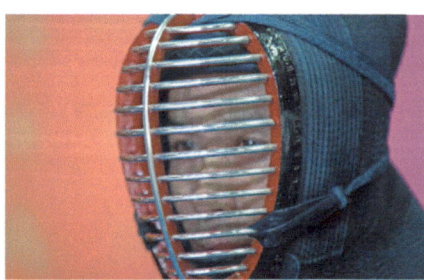

MEIJI SHRINE KOBUDŌ DEMONSTRATIONS

By Jeff Broderick

November 3, Culture Day in Japan, is well known to kendo enthusiasts around the world as it is the day of the All Japan Kendo Championships. However, it is not the only big martial arts event to be held on that day. Every year, representatives from schools of *koryū bujutsu* (old schools of martial arts) come together on the grounds of the Meiji Shrine in central Tokyo to give demonstrations of their various arts as a kind of offering to the Shinto deities. *Kendo World* was there to bring you some highlights from this day of traditional fighting arts of Japan.

Shintō Musō-ryū Jōjutsu

Shintō Musō-ryū is the leading style of *jō-jutsu* (4-foot staff) in Japan, and is closely associated with the All Japan Kendo Federation Jodo, the 12 Seitei Jodo techniques having been adopted from Shintō Musō-ryū techniques. Famously, the school was founded by Musō Gonnosuke, a renowned swordsman of the Shintō-ryū, who lost a duel with Miyamoto Musashi. Withdrawing to a mountain temple to contemplate his loss and engage in ascetic training, he received a vision of how to defeat a sword using a staff, and thus founded Shintō Musō-ryū.

Tennen Rishin-ryū

Founded in the late 18th century, Tennen Rishin-ryū's most famous practitioner was its 4th headmaster, Kondō Isami, who was famous as the head of the Shinsengumi and feared as a matchless swordsman. The school's curriculum includes *iai-jutsu*, *ken-jutsu* (seen here), *bō-jutsu*, and *jū-jutsu*.

Araki-ryū

Araki-ryū is a *sōgō bujutsu* (comprehensive martial art) which comprises techniques for *iaijutsu*, *kenjutsu*, *jūjutsu*, *bōjutsu*, *sōjutsu* (spear—shown here) and others including chain and rope weapons. Its techniques are very practical and straightforward in appearance.

Tatsumi-ryū

Often considered a school of *iai*, Tatsumi-ryū is another *ryūha* which is actually a *sōgō būjutsu*, with many weapon arts contained in its curriculum. One of these is *shuriken-jutsu*, or projectile throwing. As this sequence demonstrates, *shuriken* could have been concealed on one's person, and then thrown to injure (or at the very least distract) an opponent, at which point the fatal blow could be delivered.

Yagyū Shingan-ryū

Yagyū Shingan-ryū was quite well represented at this year's demonstration, with a number of groups from different branches of the school. This group is demonstrating techniques used between armoured opponents. This demonstration seems to represent those techniques which might be employed by lower-ranking *ashigaru* using a peasant weapon (the *kama*, or sickle) against a higher-status warrior armed with a *tachi*.

Tamiya-ryū Iaijutsu

The Tamiya-ryū school of sword-drawing was founded by Tamiya Heibei, a student of Hayashizaki Jinsuke Shigenobu. Many students of Hayashizaki and Tamiya branched off in subsequent generations and developed their own schools of *iai*, leading to a flourishing of *iai ryūha* across Japan.

Katori Shintō-ryū

One of the oldest schools of swordsmanship in Japan, Katori Shintō-ryū is renowned for its long and complex *kata*, which were designed to obscure the true significance of the movements and prevent outside observers from stealing the techniques. Born in the Warring States period during the fifteenth and sixteenth centuries, the techniques are highly practical and are designed to exploit weak points in the armour, such as inside the wrist and the throat.

Shin Musō Hayashizaki-ryū Iaijutsu

Another school which developed out of the teachings of Hayashizaki Jinsuke Shigenobu, Shin Musō Hayashizaki-ryū Iaijutsu is notable for its techniques which begin with two closely seated opponents, *uchidachi* armed with a short sword, and *shidachi* armed with an *ōdachi* (long sword).

Shin Gyōtō-ryū Kenjutsu

During the Edo period (1603–1868), there were considered to be four "great *kenjutsu* dojo": the Hokushin Ittō-ryū dōjō led by Chiba Shūsaku, the Kyōshin Meichi-ryū dojo of Momonoi Sunzo, the Shindō Munen-ryū dojo of Saitō Yakuro, and that of the Shin Gyōtō-ryū, led by eighth generation master Iba Gunbei. The school teaches a variety of *kenjutsu* techniques including *nitō* (two-sword) techniques.

Takeda-ryū Yabusame

The original weapon of the samurai was not the sword, but the bow. Takeda-ryū preserves the mounted archery of the late Heian period by performing the ritual of Yabusame, firing at targets while at full gallop, as a form of offering to the gods.

Takeda-ryū

Takeda-ryū Jingai-jutsu is the art of using a conch shell for battlefield signalling. Armies throughout history have utilised horns, trumpets, drums, and other instruments to coordinate massed troop movements. In Japan, this was often accomplished using a conch shell, and Takeda-ryū is a surviving example of these techniques. Members of the school demonstrated various signalling patterns utilising the eerie wail of the shell.

The 10th ASEAN Kendo Tournament
—Taikai Report

By Blake Bennett

Contested over two humid mid-August days in Penang, Malaysia, *Kendo World* was on site to cover the 10th ASEAN Kendo Tournament from August 23–25, 2013. Hosted by the Penang Kendo Club, a collaborative effort of members from the entire Malaysia Kendo Association (MKA) was necessary to organise and execute a *taikai* consisting of over 150 competitors from eight countries of the Association of Southeast Asian Nations (ASEAN) alliance.

Inaugurated in 1988, the ASEAN Kendo Tournament (AKT) has been hosted on Malaysian soil a total of five times to date. According to the history books, the AKT was conducted annually for a number of years from its inception. After experiencing a short lull through the late '90s, the AKT found full traction from 2001 and has been hosted consistently on a triennial basis ever since.

In its first year, the AKT was hosted in Kuala Lumpur, Malaysia, and was contested by Singapore, Thailand and the host nation. Nowadays, 25 years on, glory at the AKT is fiercely fought over by an ever growing number of kendoka from a much larger group of ASEAN countries. The growth of this year's event demanded a greater contribution from the All Japan Kendo Federation (AJKF) and the International Kendo Federation (FIK), with a delegation of officials sent to assist and oversee the refereeing. The participation of *shimpan* from a number of countries, including Hong Kong, was also acknowledged and welcomed by Professor Datuk Abdullah Malim Baginda, President of the MKA.

The total number of attendees at the 2013 event was estimated to be in excess of 300, inclusive of *shimpan* and support crew. The 10th AKT Organising Committee

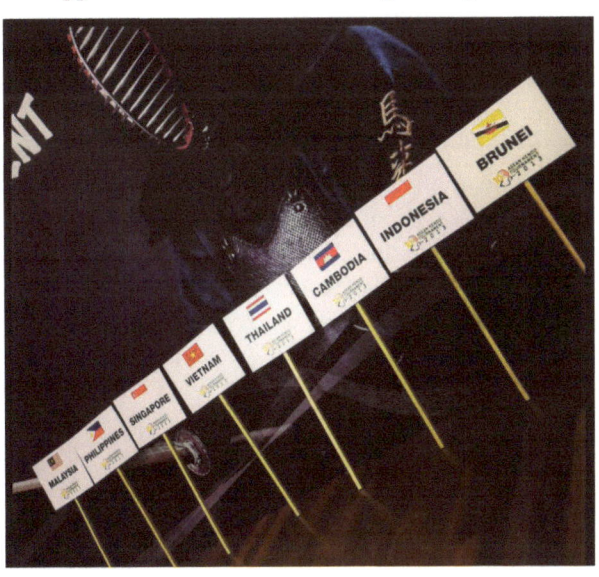

member and Penang Kendo Club advisor, Emi Yamazaki, together with WeiNien Ooi, tells KW that over 50 volunteer staff dedicated their time to manage the kendo masses from all over Southeast Asia.

> "We had initially planned for an event with 200 people, as all the facilities such as the hall, the hotel, the restaurant, the manpower, were really only able to cater for that number. So when we found out less than a month before the event that the registered number of participants was 50% more than expected, we had to go into overdrive to confirm the extra rooms, buses, and restaurant."

Not strictly limited to *shiai*, participants, officials and other guests of the 10th AKT were treated to an exhibition of *bōgu* making during the event, in addition to a raft of other cultural shows during the Sayonara Party at the hands of the organising committee.

According to Christopher Wong, secretary of the MKA, Head of the Organising Committee, and 10th AKT Tournament Director, the logistics of hosting a growing event such as this proved to be difficult in a city with a limited number of suitable venues. Wong reflects, "Once the decision was made to host the 10th AKT in Penang, the issue of sourcing an ideal venue big enough to accommodate an event of this size, with proper amenities to suit our needs, and with appropriate flooring, posed the biggest hurdle for us initially." The ideal venue was found at the Universiti Sains Malaysia (USM), a stunning campus that had previously served as barracks for the British Far East Command.

In 2008, Penang (George Town)—also referred to as the Pearl of the Orient—was proudly recognised as a UNESCO World Heritage Site, with a unique architectural and cultural townscape unparalleled in East and Southeast Asia. Yet, as Wong points out,

> "Penang is about 350km away from KL, where many of the main organisers were based, so at times it was the frequent and long travelling to and from committee meetings, plus the 'education' process for the local Penang Kendo Club, which had no experience in organising and handling an event this size, that added to the challenge. Fortunately, the MKA always had support from the regional kendo federations, as well as from the FIK and AJKF, so in this way most of the challenges were made a lot easier."

No stranger to the behind-the-scenes madness of organising an international tournament, Wong reveals that his selection to head the Organising Committee of the 10th AKT was in part due to his previous experience as Tournament Director of the 7th AKT, held in Kuala Lumpur, 2004. "Of course, the 7th AKT was on a smaller scale, so looking back it was a piece of cake in comparison!" laughs Wong.

But it was worth it. Two months on from the biggest kendo tournament ever held in Malaysia, Wong affirms that considerable press coverage and the Penang state government's involvement and support of the tournament, significantly boosted awareness of kendo in Malaysia. Wong commented that "Kendo, as in other parts of the world, is not as well known in Malaysia as other mainstream martial arts. As the 10th AKT was also highlighted through social media networks, we (the MKA) have received more inquiries about kendo and its training facilities than ever before."

Yamazaki adds, "The bottom-line is that the delegates and

competitors really enjoyed themselves, so much so that they've said they'd like to have another event in Penang!"

Results of the 10th ASEAN Kendo Tournament
Both representing Malaysia, good friends and teammates, A. Sabri and N. Amirudin, pushed through the competition to meet in the finals of the Women's Individual event. *Kote* was the *ippon* of choice for both players, with Sabri scoring two to Amirudin's one. A good match to watch as both players worked hard to overcome their familiarity with each other's fighting style.

Women's Individuals:
   1st—A Sabri (Malaysia)
   2nd—N Amirudin (Malaysia)
   3rd—D Wong (Singapore)
   3rd—G Lim (Singapore)

In a similar state of affairs to the Men's Team final, Malaysia and Singapore battled it out for bragging rights in the Women's Team event. With one win apiece and a draw in the Chūken fight, it was again a shining performance from the Malaysian aces, A. Sabri and N. Amirudin, that would assure Malaysia's victory. Final score—three wins, one loss, and one draw to Malaysia.

Women's Teams:
   1st—Malaysia A
   2nd—Singapore A
   3rd—Singapore B
   3rd—Thailand A

For many of the young guns of ASEAN kendo, victory in the Men's Individual event is a chance to exhibit the fruits of many hours of tough training in one's own country, and abroad in Japan. The climb up the competition ladder to this coveted title was, of course, dotted with plenty of entertaining upsets and comebacks. In the end, it was a blindingly fast *kote*, and equally impressive *dō* strike, that ensured victory for M. Shii of Thailand over T. Tran of Vietnam in the final match.

Mens Individuals:
1st—M Shii (Thailand)
2nd—T H Tran (Vietnam)
3rd—T A Dao (Vietnam)
3rd—R Wong (Malaysia)

The Men's Team event was concluded with a hard fought match between Singapore "A" and the host nation, Malaysia "A". While the score board suggests a convincing win by Singapore, there was no shortage of nail biting moments. Final score—three wins, two draws to Singapore.

Mens Teams:
   1st—Singapore (A)
   2nd—Malaysia (A)
   3rd—Indonesia (A)
   3rd—Malaysia (B)

The AKT has reached a level of participation that continues to exceed previous years—a positive sign for those working to promote kendo throughout Southeast Asia. And, while obviously challenging at times, the organisation and coordination of every party concerned was masterfully handled by the MKA. As with any event of this size or bigger, sailing is rarely smooth. Yet, as far as the spectators, players and officials were concerned, the 10th AKT went off without a hitch. The bar has been set. Preparation will undoubtedly begin soon for the 11th AKT in Bangkok, Thailand, where another shot at the glory of an AKT championship title awaits the kenshi of the ASEAN countries.

Looking at the History and Future of Japanese
WOMEN'S KENDO

By Ozawa Hiroshi
Translated by Kate Sylvester

Ozawa Hiroshi-sensei (K8-dan) is author of *Kendo: The Definitive Guide.* Since April 2011, he has contributed a series of monthly articles titled "Joshi Kendō no Rekishi to Kadai" (History and Issues of Women's Kendo) to *Gekkan Budō* (*Monthly Budo Magazine*). This is a translation of the 25th article in the series. It is a summary of the previous 24, and was published in the May 2013 issue of *Gekkan Budō*.

The Origin of Kendo

Kendo's techniques were basically for killing, and that means that we are using killing techniques every day in *keiko*. However, because kendo has been elevated to a "Way", they have been able to survive and remain relevant in today's society. As a result, women have been able to enter what was traditionally a "man's world" and do *keiko* with them, and now kendo is flourishing.

When you consider that the basis of kendo lies in techniques of "killing" an opponent, how are we able to reconcile that in contemporary society? It seems to be a great contradiction that practising kendo can contribute to improving one's wisdom and strength. In response to this contradiction, I came to a realisation through trial and error and repeated *keiko.*, and also because of the Great East Japan Earthquake, which occurred on March 11, 2011. The following passage was published in the introduction of my second article in the series "History and Issues of Women's Kendo" (May, 2011 *Gekkan Budō*).

"The greatest impression that remains with me was the calm acceptance of the situation, and the quiet composure shown by almost all of the people who were affected by the disaster. I have seen television reports depicting scenes of people screaming and shouting in despair when a disaster of a similar magnitude occurred overseas. However, the people of the Tohoku area appeared to accept their sad circumstances and were exceptionally calm and quiet. There was no looting of supermarkets and convenience stores to speak of—people still queued up in an orderly fashion to shop. I wonder where this strength of mind comes from. How were they able to stay so calm?"

In the June edition of the *Shinchō 45*

magazine last year, I had a discussion with Uchida Tatsuru called "Dialogue on Bushido". I shared his opinion that, "When one encounters a crisis, 'courage' is the most important thing for survival."

"The type of strength necessary to live through an ordeal is not just speed or physical power. In a crisis, it is not muscles, a strong build, or reflexes that will get you through—it is courage."

The kind of strength fostered through kendo is the ability to maintain a calm state of mind when faced with adversity. Or, it is emotional control that is demonstrated through such mundane things as not showing pleasure or joy to opponents or spectators when you win in a match. If you are awarded a point in a kendo match and you raise your fist in celebration, the point will be rescinded. This characteristic is not so common in other budo or sports. Not showing your emotions, keeping them hidden inside while exhibiting consideration for your opponent, is a traditional virtue. It links to the ability to confront problems without surprise or fear, and with a calm manner and grit.

So, with these points in mind, the themes I will address in this article are, "What should women's kendo aim for?" and, "What sort of character should women seek through doing kendo?" Simply put, I believe the answer to this question is to forge "*tanryoku*", or courage.

It is not physical strength or power; it is about performing to the maximum of your ability. Even if you possess a high degree of physical ability, this can fail to have an impact when facing an opponent if you are overcome by any one of the "four sicknesses" (surprise, fear, doubt, hesitation). They can cause your body to become immobile. While their kendo may not be particularly strong, people who are making great efforts to confront these "sicknesses" can be said to be studying true kendo.

Kendo today is different to what it was in the pre-war period. Actually, I was born in the post-war period, so I may not be qualified to comment. Still, because society has become affluent and stable, kendo has changed and more importance is placed on winning competitions rather than as a way of forging spirit and body to overcome hard times.

What Should Women's Kendo Aim For?

Enriching the heart

What sorts of people are able to grow in kendo? A person who reached the pinnacle of his profession once remarked, "Honest people grow." The word 'grow' does not simply mean improving one's skill in kendo. It also encompasses growing mentally. This growth is not necessarily visible on the outside, but you can gain an impression of someone's progression through direct contact with them.

The late Yonenaga Kunio was a highly competitive *shōgi* (Japanese chess) master. He said, "Luck will not come to those people who harbour feelings of envy, jealousy, self-pity, bitterness and hatred." Your environment and destiny change through the act of following your heart. If your heart is corrupted, your environment and destiny will become so, too. The heart or mind is one of the biggest determinants in a person's life.

What is women's kendo seeking?

I asked Kajiyama Takeko-sensei, a board member of the All Japan Naginata Federation, "Along with the development of women's kendo, what is the best way for women to be able to continue kendo? For example, how should a housewife balance housework and kendo?" She replied, "There is no simple answer to those questions. Naginata has been practised by women for much longer than kendo, and I think that an answer of sorts can be found in the naginata experience."

Kajiyama-sensei was a member of the celebrated Kōdōgikai dojo and also practised kendo there in the junior club. As this was before the war, she was told, "Because you are a girl, you must study naginata." She stopped kendo and continued naginata ever since. She must have been one of the very few women who practised kendo in the early Shōwa period (1926-1989).

Keiko from the age of 3½

It is at about 3½ years of age that you start to gain insight as an individual. I thought it inconceivable to think that a child of 3½ could practice naginata, so I asked Kajiyama-sensei the kind of training she engaged in.

"In those days, children's *keiko* started with training in front of the mirror without a *naginata*, practising footwork and body movements similar to kendo, and also how to rotate the hips and move the body while making cutting motions with the hands. From the age of 3½, I was taught naginata in this way by Hanshi Higashi Tomoko-sensei and others.

One more memory I have is how we used to clean the dojo floor. Nowadays we wipe the floor in a straight line, but at the Kōdōgikai we lined up in one row across the dojo and cleaned the floor whilst moving backwards moving from left to right diagonally across the floor. In order to 'polish our hearts', we would shout "*eitō eitō*" while zigzagging left and right as we cleaned. In the winter we had to break the ice in the buckets to be able to draw out water. With our hands red from the chill we cleaned the floors with a freezing cold cloth. When I think about it now, we were training our legs and hips without realising it. We would gradually be introduced to *keiko* actually using a *naginata*, but with one shortened to match our height. We also practised for three hours, even as 3½ year olds."

Kajiyama-sensei added that the goals for establishing the Kōdōgikai *naginata-jutsu* division were,

"First, to cultivate spiritual strength

to be resolute in the face of adversity; second, to build strong physiques in preparation for becoming the next generation of mothers. In the Kōdōgikai *naginata-jutsu* division, notable noblewomen such as Duchess Tokugawa, Duchess Yamauchi and Baroness Suwa, and a large number of other women made great efforts in running *keiko*. These women also entertained ideals of 'correcting the world' which had become quite used to luxury. They aimed to achieve this through giving students at women's schools such as Seikei, Jissen and Gakushuin, and the daughters of nobles a hard spiritual education through naginata. Furthermore, added to the cultivation and training of feminine virtues, was the development of a strong physical constitution. Naginata from the Taishō period (1912-1926) to the early part of the Shōwa period was generally learned by women from wealthy families to toughen them up."

The nature of instructors
Kajiyama-sensei commented that it is important for women when they practise budo to respect their training partner's character, and show consideration towards them during practice.

"Mothers and grandmothers have a social obligation to bring up children in a way that they become capable members of society. As an instructor, applying the same feeling in your teaching will gradually rub off on the students, who will ideally be able to make a contribution to society. Because children grow up following their parents' lead, especially that of their mother in Japan, parents must always behave appropriately."

Kajiyama-sensei discussed the requirements for being an instructor, and said that no matter how strong a teacher's kendo may be, he or she should not be followed if they are of bad character. That is to say, first and foremost in naginatakendo is the ideal of "character development". Students will encounter various problems at home or at school. If you investigate the root of the problems, you will see that is has something to do with the parent's education and discipline. Often, the parent's attitude can be the cause of a child's problems. The foundations of one's life are forged in the home.

Gender equality is gradually becoming the norm in Japan, but the relationship between sempai and kohai, regardless of gender, is problematic in many ways. It makes people lazy. Higashi Tomoko-sensei, even at the age of 85, never let people carry her things for her. Higashi-sensei is a great instructor in the naginata world, and even if you offered to carry her bags she would reply, "It's okay young man", and carry them herself. There are times and circumstances when people will offer to do things for you, but I think it best to say, "I will do it myself, but thank you for offering."

However, this trend is not particularly strong in Japan. In the U.K., I have seen many university cricket, rugby and soccer club practices and competitions, and have spoken with the players. I have never once seen a kohai wash a sempai's uniform or carry their belongings. Should this be something that is approved of in terms of the process of learning? When such an action is done purely out of kindness, I think it is fine to sometimes relent and let the person do it. On the other hand, if someone does not desire it, it should not be forced or done simply out of a sense of obligation. It is good when a student wants to show respect to a sensei voluntarily, but it is unacceptable if the teacher or sempai expects this to be done. Such behaviour should not be used as the basis for deciding if a child or person is "good" or not. Unfortunately though, this is often the case.

The teacher-student relationship
A student can look at a teacher and think, "I can respect that person as my teacher"; but it is a big mistake for a teacher to look at someone and think, "That person is my student." Humans are born equal. People make great efforts throughout their lives to acquire various skills; they may start to rise above others, and become a person of noble character. Naturally, others may come to respect them, which is not a bad thing at all. If someone becomes an instructor before their character has developed adequately, however, even if they espouse the same tenets of wisdom as an experienced instructor, they will unfortunately come across as being forceful. Of course, a teacher must be technically proficient, but they must also have maturity to be respected.

This maturity enables a teacher to know how to instruct each student according to their needs. Women kendoka now have many opportunities to see men's competitions, and there are countless co-ed schools where male and female students practise together. Women's kendo has essentially developed through training together with men, and often it is men who teach them. It is becoming increasingly necessary for instructors to understand the differences in psychology between males and females.

The purpose of kendo for young students
What is the duty of a young student? Firstly, a kendo practitioner still at school should never neglect his or her studies. What are called "club activities" in Japan are extracurricular activities that are done after lessons. I tell young students that if they have time, they should practise; but if they neglect studies and work hard only at their club activity, then their priorities are wrong. Ideally, it is important for young students to work hard both in study and club activities as a healthy body is important for withstanding the rigours of school work. At least, that's what I encourage my students to strive for regardless of their gender.

The future direction of women's kendo
One of my teachers once said to me that when you are so busy with your work and you cannot practise kendo. You must then put all of your effort and focus on your

work, and forget about kendo. If you want to continue kendo throughout your life, it is important to balance it with your work. Yamaguchi-sensei made the following three suggestions:

"First, tend to your health. If you catch a cold, have a sore stomach, or sprain an ankle, you cannot practise kendo. Never neglect your health. This is the first step towards being able to do things yourself. Second, tend to the health of your family. If you want to practise kendo regularly, the condition of your family's health determines your lifestyle. Therefore, if your husband or child is sick, you should not go to kendo. Third, if your work is not going well, you should not practise kendo."

Only after you have completely satisfied these three points, she asserts, can you take time to go to kendo. Kendo comes fourth. Women can practise kendo freely when they are students and have no family obligations. "If child rearing is not taken seriously, the child's growth can be hindered."

While Karume Michiyo (K7-dan) was a school teacher between 1992 and 1993, she had to manage her classes, teach P.E., instruct at the kendo club, raise her children, and take care of the housework. Through all of this pressure, she became ill to the point where she felt her life was in danger. She overcame her illness with the help of her husband and family. For women to continue kendo throughout their lives, they need the understanding and cooperation of their families.

The Future of Women's Kendo

Will there be a female 8-dan?
In the summer of 2012, a female kenshi from Australia asked me, "Why are there no female 8-dan?" I gave the following answer. Each *dan* grade has its own respective level of *shingitai* (spirit, technique and body). For example *shodan* has its own

balance of experience and *shingitai*, as does 5-dan. Similarly, I think that there is a balance of experience, level of training and *shingitai* required for only 8-dan. If you do not have a level of *shingitai* that is more than adequate, you will not pass.

Now, women and men take grading exams together. In order to pass 8-dan your *shingitai* needs to be complete; and if it is, you will pass on the first time. To take the exam you must be at least 46 years of age, but there is a big gap between women's and men's strength that needs to be conciliated. If a woman was to pass 8-dan, she would be required to be *motodachi* for people who were attempting the 8-dan grading. Those people may include men who have won the All Japan Kendo Championships. It may be beneficial to practise with such people, but there is a risk of injury when doing *taiatari*, for example. If an injury occurs, you cannot say, "I got hurt as a result of being knocked down by your strong *taiatari*." No matter who comes to practise with you, even if you are injured, you cannot make excuses.

Thus, in order for women to be able to pass the 8-dan examination, it is necessary to devise a method of *keiko* with men who are significantly stronger physically. When that type of kendo is discovered, I think a new, wonderful era of women's kendo will be born. From now, the task at hand is to start research and discussion with our female colleagues on this very matter.

Information for 8-dan Grading

This is an extract of the Kendo Grading Regulations (June 24, 1999) for 8-dan.

Required Standard
Article 14
   An 8-dan must have mastered the secrets of kendo, exhibit maturity and have perfect technique.

Eligibility Requirements
Article 16
   A candidate must have held 7-dan for more than 10 years and be at least 46 years of age.

Determining Success or Failure
Article 18
   To pass the first practical examination, four or more of the examiners must agree to pass the candidate; in the

second practical assessment, six or more must agree to pass the candidate. In the first practical examination there are six examiners; in the second there are nine.

Potential issues regarding physical differences in men and women

I was taken aback when I observed the practical component of a 4- and 5-dan grading in Tokyo recently. Men and women grade together, but there is clearly a difference in strength, build and athletic dexterity. I watched in fear that an unexpected accident would occur. For example, when a woman of small stature attempts to strike a powerful man's *men*, he may deflect the attack and knock the woman over with *taiatari*. This is something I have witnessed many times in the past. There have been numerous cases where women have been flipped over backwards, landing on their heads, and suffered concussion. This also happens when men fight each other, but that women have to be especially careful. Compared to regular practice, people are tense and use more power in a grading. There is often excess force used in *taiatari*, and unnecessary pushing with the arms.

A few years ago, an English acquaintance of mine came to Japan to take the 6-dan grading in Nagoya, and I went along with him to watch. That Englishman was 195cm tall and weighed 100kg. At that time he was 50 years old, but during his high school years he was a rugby player and did judo as a university student. In the grading, one of his opponents was male and the other was a woman who was only 150cm tall. I watched the match with great interest wondering how it would turn out. When the woman made a *men* cut, he blocked it with his *shinai*, and he pushed a little with his arms against her *taiatari* and sent her flying back five metres where she fell over. I spoke with him afterwards and he said, "I didn't push with excessive force, I only responded to my opponent's *taiatari*."

Some issues for women in kendo

It is important that from now the number of female instructors increases. This is because women can better understand women's issues. From an instructor's perspective, women teachers cannot rely on others but must be confident in their ability, and have conviction to move kendo forward. What is their goal? Is it to win *shiai*? Is it to grade? Women, as with men, should have clear ambitions in their kendo. They should be motivated for competition and gradings, and eventually, they should aspire to challenge for 8-dan. Is the goal to foster one's spirit, to maintain health, and cultivate physical strength, or to cultivate discipline? It is all of these things. I would like to end this article with a quote from Tamamoto Kenkichi's explanation of Inoue Yasushi's book *Tenpyō no Iraka*.

"Human activity, which must appear the same as the comings and goings of ants in the eyes of the gods, becomes totally shrouded in the mists of time. What determines the significance or insignificance of a human deed goes infinitely beyond human intention. Human history, after all, is based on countless human actions that appear to have no meaning whatsoever in the grand scheme of things. The truth about human beings is, even if you know some action or deed might be absolutely pointless, you cannot help but to do it anyway. The monks described in *Tenpyo no Iraka*, who left Japan's shores to study Buddhist Law in China and spent their entire time transcribing a sutra to bring back to Japan, ended up drowning at sea together with the copies of the sutra. Perhaps they were aware that their training and the fruits of their labours would be futile, but still, they had no choice but to try."

Kendo practice and activities are somewhat similar to this. "Do what you can as a human being with your own free will, even if it may bear no fruit." I believe all kendo practitioners, regardless of gender, need to have such determination. The walls between the sexes in kendo are slowly coming down, but there is still so much to do. Every drop in the bucket helps.

Kendo That Cultivates People

by Sumi Masatake (Hanshi 8-dan)
Translated by Honda Sōtarō

Part 15
Teaching Kendo to the Next Generation (Part 1)

We have come a long way in this series of articles and are near the final stage. However, looking back on the content thus far, I acknowledge that there is much I need to reconsider. Most of the content has been about training and teaching methodology with a large focus on the acquisition of techniques. I realise now that my examination into 'the principles of the *katana*' as outlined in "The Concept of Kendo" and my examination of character building through kendo were both insufficient. In an intellectual sense I have stated that kendo training should not merely be about the pursuit of technical proficiency and success in competition, but, to my great surprise, I feel as if I have fallen into a rut in my own teaching approach. In my fervent attempts to instruct on the technical and physical aspects of kendo, I fear that I have overlooked the greater objectives of kendo training. Therefore, in this installment, I will discuss how to recognise the objectives of kendo training through the act of teaching.

Kendo through teaching and teaching through kendo

I attended a symposium for the improvement of kendo instruction in Fukuoka Prefecture in August 1989. It was held to coincide with the 31st All Japan Teachers Kendo Championship. I always remember an interesting comment made by H8-dan Iwatani Fumio of Akita Prefecture in response to a younger teacher's question during one of the panel discussions. The question posed to Iwatani Sensei was, "Your school's kendo team have won the national championships and regularly rank highly in the All Japan Inter-High School Kendo Championship. How did you teach and train such strong competitors?" Iwatani Sensei replied, "I was never aware that I was teaching my students kendo and I don't think I am even now!" Naturally all those present were perplexed by this answer. Iwatani sensei went on to clarify, "But I can assure you that I have trained hard with my students; this is what was instilled into me when I was a student at the Tōkyō Kōtō Shihan Gakkō (Tokyo Higher Normal School). The famous instructors who taught there did not explain or demonstrate *waza* to their students. Even the senior students, who were already quite experienced, did their best to strike the instructors during *keiko*, but the instructors' *kamae* would be too strong and students would generally find the *kensen* at their throat. They would often lose balance and fall to the floor after being evaded by one of the instructors or they would be rammed into a wall after receiving a powerful *tsuki*. Seeing the senior students helpless against the instructors made me think about what it means to be strong in kendo. I resigned myself to attacking with big and straight *men* strikes. The school's instructors did not teach me how to strike *men* quickly or how to use my hips when striking; they taught me to fully commit myself physically and mentally to every attack and to not be afraid of my opponent's *kensen*. Tricks or cunning tactics had no effect on them. This taught me that I have to face every opponent with 100 per cent resolve and put everything I have into each strike." I was 44 years old at the time that I was chairing this symposium and I found myself very moved by Iwatani-sensei's comments. I started to reconsider my own approach to teaching kendo to students, because I was always focused on aspects of attacking and counterattacking and lectured my students on *maai*, timing and tactics. I realised that in teaching kendo to students I should foster in them a firm spirit of resolve; a spirit so strong that they will not shy away from difficulties or fear. I do not know how many of the young teachers at the symposium fully understood Iwatani-sensei's comments, but I believe that the essence of kendo training lies in developing bravery and perseverance to overcome adversity. Even though times are changing and practitioners tend to focus on competitions, it is important that we maintain this essence.

Kendo instructors must vary the difficulty of *keiko* according to their students' physical abilities, technical skill and levels of motivation. Students should not be overworked nor subject to harsh or unreasonable treatment. At the *nyūmon-ki* stage it is important to build up students' mental attitudes first. Beginners may be frivolous in their approach to training and the instructor may need to lead by example in cultivating an appropriate attitude in accordance with students' levels of progress. It is not easy to learn or to teach someone how to be brave in the face of difficulty.

Most people usually underestimate their mental and physical limits; even if they get to a stage at which they think they cannot go on any further, they usually can, as they have not reached their true limits yet. Real self-development comes from daring to push those supposed limits even further. The decision to push oneself this far should come from within the individual and not from an external source. In teaching kendo to the next generation, students must be made to repeatedly attack; it is through this experience they will benefit from the training process and absorb the cultural value of *keiko*. The essence of kendo can be found in overcoming the difficulty experienced in acquiring correct sword handling and technical skills. It is not found in blindly obeying the stipulations of one individual instructor.

In western Fukuoka City, there is a profound dojo motto which hangs on the wall of the Kitazaki Children's Kendo Club: "When faced with difficulty, dare to take one step forward." Fukuoka was rocked by a powerful earthquake on March 10, 2005. The epicentre was close to the western area of the city and many houses, farms, and sporting and fishing facilities were badly damaged. Only six months after the earthquake, the Kitazaki Children's Kendo Club successfully held a *taikai* for the 10th anniversary of the founding of their dojo. They added an extra subscript to the name of their tournament: "With prayers for a quick recovery from the earthquake". I

believe that both locals and non-locals that were involved in the *taikai* must have learned a great deal through their participation. The true essence of kendo is embodied in that motto: "When faced with difficulty, dare to take one step forward."

Many people lament that the future of Japan is in jeopardy because they believe that the youth of today have lost their strength of will, are physically weak, and do not perform well academically when compared with previous generations. I believe, however, that there is a ray of a hope; if the bravery and perseverance to overcome adversity can be instilled into the hearts of youth today then they will develop passionate minds, strong bodies, and sound intellects. We should feel proud of the culture we are imparting to students when teaching kendo as we are cultivating the next generation who will be responsible for the future of kendo.

Mutual learning through the student-teacher relationship

I was appointed as the chief referee for the final match of the 53rd All Japan Kendo Championship in November 2005. The final was fought between Uchimura Ryōichi, a new contender at age 25, and Harada Satoru, a veteran who at age 32 had appeared many times in previous championships but had always lost by narrow margins. Both of them belong to the Tokyo Metropolitan Police Force and neither of them held back in the match. They both demonstrated excellent kendo and all of the 8000 audience members' eyes were riveted to the action.

The match went into overtime and Harada applied strong *seme* and scored a beautiful *debana-kote* when Uchimura tried to strike *men*. It was a thrilling and impressive end to the final match and a thunder of applause arose from the audience. The audience was cheering for his success but also for him coming back to win after having been runner-up in the previous year's championship. When the winner's interview began in the middle of the arena, no one got up to leave. Harada's first words were, "Thank you very much to everyone! I can't thank you enough!" The audience erupted into another massive round of applause at his words. He had made a sensational debut in his first entry into the Championship when, at the tender age of 23, he took 2nd-place. Although he was obviously a strong contender and had won prizes in five of his eight appearances, he had never actually taken 1st-place. This time he won and I was impressed by the manner in which he immediately thanked his teachers, work superiors and colleagues, and his family for all of their support. I was honoured to be the chief referee for this *shiai* and I felt he had demonstrated an exemplary model of kendo spirit to the kendo community.

Via a press release, I later learned how he had put his emotions in order after losing in the final of the previous Championship and returned to his training with a firm resolve. I imagined the sincerity with which people around him were willing him to win. Giving the first word of thanks to those who supported him showed great humility and the kendo community can be proud of this excellent role model. Harada should be praised for showing great courage under enormous pressure and devoting himself tirelessly to his goal, however his modest attitude, as shown through his comments, deserves even more praise. It was a special moment when those present in the arena and those watching from afar all cheered together in their support of his achievements.

Harada Satoru's victory aside, we can surmise that kendo is a form of culture in which we analyse human relationships through the close interplay of personalities that occurs when people face each other in *keiko*. Therefore the aims that instructors set for their students and their objectives in teaching are very important. It would be absurd to try to teach techniques by word alone, or speak of the cultivation of character in a solely intellectual way without physically engaging students. Teachers should be aware and teachers should make students realise that true cultivation of the character is only achieved through hard training. There is much more to be gained through hard training than mastery of technique. Ideally, personal interaction between teachers and students will foster courage under pressure, a zest for life, courtesy, gratitude and modesty.

The late Nakayama Hakudō Hanshi placed an emphasis on the notion of *shi-tei-dō-gyō*, which means that master and pupil should learn from each other as they are on the same path. I try to be a considerate instructor because I believe that students are a reflection of their teachers; they will inadvertently mimic their teacher's weaknesses while taking much longer to acquire their teacher's strengths. The behaviour and performance of students during training is usually a reaction to the style of teaching of their instructor. However, the only way to learn how to teach is by teaching, and instructors need patience in this regard. If a teacher displays a conscientious attitude then students will respond positively to this and it will contribute to their character development. Instructors need to push their students hard in training, but the educational benefits of *keiko* increase when the instructor fosters students' characters as well.

A relationship of *shi-tei-dō-gyō* is not transient, as in the workplace or an organisation, nor is it based on experience and grade; it is a mutual attitude or feeling that comes from the heart. An instructor should not be overconfident in their teaching capacity nor should they be boastful or show off their skills. An instructor must be determined to work hard to bring out their students' potential. If relationships of this nature can be formed and made manifest in kendo, then the cultural value that kendo offers will appeal to society at large. If not, we risk having a large proportion of power relationships based on skill, violence and fear. Mutual learning through the student-teacher relationship cultivates virtues such as affection, courtesy, modesty, honour and sincerity, which benefit ourselves and others outside of the dojo and enrich society as a whole.

****

Japan was shocked at the end of 2005 when it was revealed that respected construction businesses had been neglecting basic design criteria in high-rise buildings. Yet again it was shocked in the 2006 New Year's period at the news that a public figure renowned for his work and considered a stock market genius had been arrested on suspicion of violating securities and exchange laws. I feel this is evidence of a recent decline in morality at the corporate level. I am alarmed when I think about the effect that these scandals must have on the youth of today considering that the individuals and groups involved have such high levels of social responsibility. Naturally having a solid administrative structure and rivals to engage you in healthy competition will foster sincerity, but you must have courage and integrity not to give in to pressure or temptation. However, a person can only make use of their abilities and talents if the group to which they belong to functions to a high standard. Kimura Tokutarō, the first president of the All Japan Kendo Federation, proposed that kendo practitioners should strive to embody the three virtues of wisdom, compassion and courage (*chi-jin-yū*). We as kendo teachers have a very important social responsibility in our task of teaching kendo to the next generation.

Fostering an independent attitude in learning techniques

Kendo training begins with the learning of individual techniques, but traditionally, when a new student joined a dojo, they were required to demonstrate a strong attitude and a voluntary acceptance of the rigours to come before they would be taught techniques. After this phase, the teacher had the student follow their lead and the examples set by seniors and, in doing so, the student would actually teach themselves; one unique characteristic of the path of swordsmanship. This method is virtually extinct nowadays, and in academia, arts and sports, methods of learning and practice have been devised through investigative research and now students are spoon-fed step-by-step.

Poor results often occur when teachers are given unrealistic teaching goals, such as teaching techniques in a short period of time. The teacher wants the students to develop a sense of independence but at the same time injury prevention is paramount. Consequently their teaching style tends to be overprotective and intrusive and effectively they 'over-teach' in their rush for results. Students feel pressured by being forced to learn and practise and experience a loss of independence. This is sometimes seen in kendo when a young practitioner who has been pushed into kendo by their parents or teachers becomes quite proficient but then suddenly quits. On the other end of the spectrum, there are also many cases where beginners lack proper basic skills and quit because they were left to their own devices by their teacher under the guise of "respecting the student's independence". In the former case of the student who did not start kendo of their own choosing, it is likely they were not able to handle pressure or cope with failure because they lacked independence in their kendo. In the latter case of the student who lacked proper basic skills, perhaps they were overconfident in their abilities despite not being technically proficient and they lost confidence once their lack of proper training was exposed. There are many reasons why a young practitioner might quit kendo, but we must keep in mind that they are generally being influenced by external factors and there is often a lack of substantial connection between their inner-self and how they are made to practise.

The practice of kendo basics involves our inner-selves and great pleasure can be experienced through managing a successful *waza*; this is one of the fascinating things about kendo. Teachers need to make their students aware that kendo is also about developing the inner-self and that this is an endless task.

The following is a three-stage breakdown of the training process of kendo which also alludes to how practitioners should train their inner-self at each stage.

Stage 1 – *shin*:

Internalising techniques such as *tai-sabaki* and *shinai-sabaki* which use the whole body as in *suburi* and *kūkan-datotsu*.

Stage 2 – *gyō*:

Correctly executing individual techniques in predetermined situations against a partner as in *kirikaeshi* and *uchikomi-geiko*.

Stage 3 – *sō*:

Refining techniques in free-sparring situations against a partner as in *gokaku-geiko* and *shiai*.

Needless to say, interpersonal techniques that form the core of kendo have both physical and mental elements. As a practitioner progresses in their training, the mental elements of technique become more important, as does individual willpower. Physical elements will not function correctly and technique acquisition will plateau unless the strength of one's will is cultivated. Simply understanding how the physical and mental elements of training are related to each other is not enough. Techniques must be practised and one's whole personality must be cultivated. Otherwise, half of the benefit of training is lost and practitioners may become disheartened and quit as in the two aforementioned cases.

To pursue techniques solely as a means to competitive success is a perversion of the path of kendo and practitioners must always strive to cultivate their personalities. The success or failure of a technique in competition is very visible and obvious, but there are many more important intangible aspects to kendo

practice. These intangible aspects must not be overlooked and practitioners should form a habit of reflecting on them from time to time.

The importance of mental training should not be underestimated

The process of technique acquisition involves hard practice and training of the emotions. Patience and self-control are also cultivated through hard training, which help the practitioner build courage. Respect is expressed through three different kinds of *rei* in the dojo: *rei* to the front, *rei* to one's teachers, and *rei* to one's training partners. These customs of respect ideally lead the practitioner to become a considerate person.

Teachers are prone to use "explanation", "instruction", and "command", but to foster introspection in students a teacher should use "suggestions", "questions", and "approval". This encourages students to examine themselves in respect to the teachings of kendo. Teachers should praise spiritual or mental growth in students because students might not have noticed it for themselves. This will strengthen their social attitude. Some students think they are fine as long as they do what they are told and that they will be punished if they do not. These kinds of passive individuals have been conditioned not to take initiative and their minds have not been able to fully develop. There is also a risk that these kinds of individuals will lose their zest for life in modern society where independence and decision-making is required of them on a daily basis.

If teachers hope to cultivate students' inner-selves, then they should not be overprotective or intrusive, nor should they over-teach their students. If the focus of kendo moves away from what is "correct" to the pursuit of "superior technique" then the essence of kendo is lost and it simply becomes a violent combat sport. Practitioners should therefore make a habit of "doing the right thing" in regular training such as performing the rituals of etiquette properly with good posture, and correctly observing the technical requirements of *suburi*, *tai-sabaki* and basic striking. Performing these actions with the correct mindset not only polishes technique, but also enhances one's inner-self, wherein lies the essence of kendo. To correctly cultivate the inner-self one must rid themselves of the notion that winning is everything and make a firm resolve to only practise with correct physical and mental posture and to only use proper *waza*. Teachers must make students aware that by practising in this manner students' personalities will be cultivated in a just way. Teachers should also acknowledge and praise students' genuine and earnest desire to improve, as this will increase their self-esteem.

If a student becomes obsessed with winning, then "doing the right thing" will seem less important to them. Although a strong desire to win is generally encouraged, it will often stunt a student's inner growth. Telling stories of famous warriors and heroic deeds of old is one good method of passing on moral teachings, but obviously there are countless instances when teachers can help their students realise the value of "doing the right thing" in the daily occurrences of training. Teachers should give a lot of thought to what kind of insightful comments they can make to their students; comments that will have an effect on their lives both inside and outside the dojo. This idea is summed up in the phrase "*kendō-soku-seikatsu*" (what we learn in kendo, we can apply in our lives).

Reconsidering the notion of "spirituality"

It seems that when people speak of "spirituality" and "willpower" their comments are often written off as old-fashioned or illogical. In sports, the expression *seishin-shugi* is often used interchangeably with *konjō-shugi* (belief in the importance of guts/fortitude), which may then be misconstrued to justify unreasonably hard training akin to bullying (*shigoki*). Hence people seem more comfortable with a phrase like "fighting spirit" and may refer to "spiritual training" as "mental training".

Many people overestimate mental training and think that with the right mental training anyone can become capable of anything. People need to be aware that top athletes who calmly perform amazing physical feats and show impressive displays of sportsmanship and attitude have generally gone through great physical, mental and emotional ordeals in order to reach their level of proficiency. Aptitude and physique aside, their willpower is what enabled them to overcome these challenges. Athletes and sportspeople do not talk of willpower that much, and it is not visible to the eyes of spectators so many overlook it. Visual and written media have played a large role in bolstering general interest in and spreading information about sports, but I believe that many people are still misinformed about psychological aspects of sports.

In kendo there is a general understanding that while we are training hard physically, we are also simultaneously developing our personality and character to become well-rounded individuals. During kendo's development there were times when enforcements of regulation were necessary to avoid too much focus being placed on one aspect of kendo or another, and often these situations were related to changes in the social circumstances of the time. The debate over the name "kendo" is an interesting example.

At the end of the Meiji period, kendo was referred to as *gekiken* or *kenjutsu*, titles that many university and technical college club members believed to be inappropriate for the swordsmanship activity that they practised.

Accordingly they joined in debates with budo professionals to update the name to better reflect their beliefs and attitudes towards the practice. They changed the names of their clubs to "kendo clubs" stating that what they do is not *gekiken* or *kenjutsu*, which are pursuits of technique, but "*kendō*" (the way of the sword), which aims to cultivate the mind. I have great respect for those students' beliefs and their tenacity. I will not discuss this debate in further detail here, but I wish to point out that, whilst considering the present situation and the future of kendo, there are many things that can be learned from the past.

Twenty-three years after the establishment of the All Japan Kendo Federation, *The Concept of Kendo* was established in 1975. The concept was formulated with the intention of correcting over-emphasis on learning techniques for competition, and contributing to the spread of kendo as an art of self-improvement. Over 30 years have passed since then but I still have doubts about the priorities of many practitioners.

The Concept of Kendo

The concept of Kendo is to discipline the human character through the application of the principles of the *katana* (sword).

The concept can easily be learned by heart and even primary and junior high school practitioners can recite it and reproduce it correctly on written tests at grading examinations. It concerns me, however, that *The Purpose of Practicing Kendo*, which was established at the same time as *The Concept of Kendo*, has not spread to the same extent.

> ***The Purpose of Practicing Kendo -***
> *The purpose of practicing Kendo is:*
> *To mold the mind and body,*
> *To cultivate a vigorous spirit,*
> *And through correct and rigid training,*
> *To strive for improvement in the art of Kendo,*
> *To hold in esteem human courtesy and honour,*
> *To associate with others with sincerity,*
> *And to forever pursue the cultivation of oneself.*
> *This will make one be able:*
> *To love his/her country and society,*
> *To contribute to the development of culture*
> *And to promote peace and prosperity among all peoples.*

These guidelines clearly set out how the practitioner may "discipline the human character" as mentioned in "The Concept of Kendo". It provides a checklist of questions that all practitioners should consider and ask of themselves. If we desire to cultivate our minds as individuals, as members of families or organisations, or as citizens in communities, countries, and the world, then "The Purpose of Practicing Kendo" outlines what we must do.

Kendo teachers should pay greater heed to "The Purpose of Practicing Kendo" and should explain to their students the importance of strengthening the mind and building a fair and strong attitude over strengthening the body.

The warrior spirit as represented in kendo has been used in the past to promote Japanese ultra-nationalism, but now people of all ages can be proud of the spiritual legacy of peace and hard work that kendo has given us. I hope that everyone can proudly use their kendo spirit to benefit themselves and those around them, both inside and outside of the dojo.

KENDO, INHERITED WISDOM AND PERSONAL REFLECTIONS

By Geoff Salmon

Review by Michael Ishimatsu-Prime

In the previous issue of *Kendo World* (6.4, June 2013), there was a review of K7-dan Geoff Salmon-sensei's *Kendo: A Comprehensive Guide to Japanese Swordsmanship* which was published by Tuttle earlier this year. Clearly not content with putting out only one book in 2013, Salmon has also released *Kendo, Inherited Wisdom and Personal Reflections*. Anyone who has read Salmon's blog—www.kendoinfo.net—will know that he writes prolifically on kendo, on a wide range of topics, and his latest book is a collection of his blog's 52 most popular posts.

Whereas *Kendo: A Comprehensive Guide to Japanese Swordsmanship* is a training manual, *Kendo, Inherited Wisdom and Personal Reflections* instead generally concentrates on the more esoteric, philosophical and cultural aspects of kendo and budo. However, that is not to say that this book is devoid of technical advice. When Salmon explains some of the practical aspects of kendo, such as *tenouchi*, *kaeshi-dō* or *hikitate-geiko*, his explanations are complemented with his personal take on the technique gained through 40-plus years of experience, and are sometimes augmented with the thoughts of other high-ranked sensei. This book is more anecdotal than what a technical manual would probably allow.

The title is made of two parts—"inherited wisdom" and "personal reflections"—and there are plenty of examples of both contained in the book's 170 pages. Some of the kendo wisdom that Salmon has inherited, and then passes on through this book, comes from such esteemed sensei as H8-dan Chiba Masashi

and H8-dan Sueno Eiji among others. Some examples are Chiba-sensei discussing *maai* (p.13-15), *chudan-no-kamae* and cutting motion (p.19-21), and Sueno-sensei talking about *suburi* (p.99-101).

Perhaps the pick of the samples of "inherited wisdom" is the first article titled "The Aim of Kendo" written by H9-dan Matsumoto Toshio-sensei (pictured below), who exhorts the reader to treat kendo with the same seriousness and purpose of mind as if it was a real fight with real swords. He also states the importance of knowing the right moments to attack, and that these moments should not be missed.

There are many personal reflections, too. Salmon writes on concepts like *fudōshin* (p.11-12), *kigurai* (p.25-26), *shu-ha-ri* (p.43-45), *kihaku* (p.47-48), and *seme* and *tame* (p.165-167) to name but a few, and as with his explanation of techniques, these go beyond a brief dictionary definition. Salmon writes about these and other topics in a clear and concise manner, sometimes with a degree of levity, and in a way that is relatable to both the beginner and experienced kendoka alike.

Kendo, Inherited Wisdom and Personal Reflections does not need to be read from start to finish, but can be dipped into depending on what you want to read about. I do not think that it would be of much use in the dojo to consult during *keiko*, but it would be very well suited to the bus ride to or from training, or in a quiet moment at home when you have no *keiko*, and are in the mood to contemplate or reflect on your kendo.

It will be interesting to see what Salmon-sensei comes up with next year.

Kendo, Inherited Wisdom and Personal Reflections (170 pages) published by Rethink Press and is available on Amazon priced at £8.43 / US$13.50

The Kendo Coach
Sports Psychology in Kendo
Part 10—Series Summary
By Blake Bennett

Over the course of the past nine articles, the "Kendo Coach" series has aimed to highlight the importance of various psychological issues within the kendo dojo.

From the first article entitled "Developing a Psychological Skills Training (PST) Programme", through to the fifth article entitled "Team Cohesion and Goal Setting", both the relevance and application of mental skills in kendo were addressed. Each article introduced a new topic concerning the demands and requirements of an athlete to enter his/her ideal performance state (IPS), and was concluded with suggested methods and resources that could assist the kendo coach to develop a broader range of skills in their athletes.

Parts 6 through 9 of the "Kendo Coach" series dealt with an equally important issue that requires the attention of kendo coaches in any and every dojo—that of violence and aggression. These articles were not accompanied by the "how to" worksheets as in previous issues. Rather, they were intended to inform the reader of the current psychological literature on the topic of aggression in sport, and thus encourage self-reflection and action wherever deemed necessary.

As a concluding piece to the "Kendo Coach" articles, part 10 will provide a brief "taster" of the entire series. To begin with, and in order of publication, the mental (PST) skills and methods that were covered will be reviewed. Further, in light of the improved availability of previous issues of the *Kendo World* journals via POD (print on demand) technology, reference will be made to the volume in which the applicable article was published—encouraging the reader to access the worksheets developed for PST training in kendo, and thus enriching one's coaching toolbox.

Following this review, the second section will synopsise the articles focused on the topic of aggression in kendo. Importantly, various considerations affecting the definitions given to aggression in contact and combat sports, and the issues specific to the kendo *keiko* environment will be revisited here.

Part 1: Developing a Psychological Skills Training (PST) Programme
Kendo World Journal 4 (4): pp. 90-95, 2009

Overview of the topic

The introductory article to this series carried out two main objectives. First, on the premise of achieving an Ideal Performance State (IPS), the article sought to justify the need for mental or psychological skills training in kendo. The second objective was to provide a resource for the kendo coach to use together with the athlete to identify which skills are in need of improvement to achieve IPS in *keiko* and *shiai*.

Often denoted as "the zone", IPS refers to the optimal physical and psychological condition for peak performance (Hodge, 2004). Simply, it is the mood, feeling or state in which an athlete feels utterly focused, both mentally and physically.

According to Hodge, the following skills and abilities represent the IPS:

- Good mental preparation (mental readiness)
- Complete concentration
- High self-confidence
- High motivation
- The ability to control activation and anxiety
- The ability to cope with pressure

The immediate hurdle that many kenshi face when entering the court, in some cases regardless of experience, is the perception that their abilities are not sufficient to meet and conquer the demands of the situation. That is, the internal voice that screams, "This is too difficult and beyond my capabilities".

The literature suggests that, in order to achieve IPS, the athlete must undergo a program of Psychological Skills Training (PST) (Hodge, 2004). The foremost intention of such a program is to assist the athlete in overcoming whatever psychological barrier he/she faces when it is time to perform well. However, due to the multitude of potential issues—whether it be nerves, concentration, confidence, or a combination of each—and the plethora of possible methods to help overcome these hurdles, it is necessary to analyse the individual athlete's needs.

Resource

In order to effectively conduct a PST programme with an athlete, it is crucial to first identify which aspects of performance need to be developed, and accordingly, the psychological skills that require attention. Analysis of this information provides the coach and athlete with a basis upon which the methods to modify the mental state can be selected. This can be achieved effectively by having the competitor respond to a series of simple needs analysis worksheets.

The needs analysis process divides ideal performance into the four key areas of technical, tactical, physical, and of course, psychological components. The worksheets therefore act as a resource for the kendo coach to identify the athlete's desire for development in aspects all across the board.

Taylor (1995), and Boutcher and Rotella (1987) emphasise the importance of structuring a PST program that aligns itself with the unique demands and characteristics of a specific sport. With this point in mind, the needs assessment task sheets provided in the first article have been adapted from the "Peak Performance Profile" and "Peak Performance Skills Worksheet" outlined by Hodge (2004), with modifications to include kendo terminology, and a number of original ideas that have been developed for use by kendo athletes specifically.

Part 2: Coping with Anxiety— an examination of arousal and anxiety and its effects on performance

Kendo World Journal, 5 (1): pp. 76-87, 2009

Overview of the topic

Anxiety is an inherent part of any competitive or evaluative situation. However, the extent to which anxiety affects an athlete's performance depends greatly on various personality and environmental factors. Burton and Raedeke (2008) suggest that many coaches incorrectly interpret an athlete's sub-par performance as a sign of poor physical preparation. This inevitably results in attempts to solve the problem with more conditioning or skill repetitions. Furthermore, even having identified a meagre performance as an issue of anxiety or arousal, some coaches may be at a loss as to how to help an athlete effectively manage and facilitate this energy expenditure for peak performance.

The sport psychology literature regarding anxiety and arousal emphasises the point that these terms are often used interchangeably, as if they were one and the same (Morris & Summers, 1995). Although each concept is closely linked in many situations, it is important to recognise that *arousal* is best understood in terms of physiological responses to stressful situations, and *anxiety* in terms of psychological obstacles the athlete faces as a result of his/her interpretation of *arousal*.

The causes of anxiety for an athlete are many. However, Jones, Swain, and Cale (1990) have identified five factors that noticeably contribute to an athlete's competitive anxiety/stress:

- Perceived readiness (or lack thereof)
- Attitude toward previous performance
- Perceived difficulty of the current task
- Coach/parental influence
- The external environment

Athletes who perform better overall tend to perceive anxiety and pressure as more facilitative to their performance than their lower performing, less competitive and less confident counterparts (Vealey, 2003). To this end, perception and interpretation of psychological and physiological states play important roles in the effective facilitation of anxiety and arousal levels.

Resources

A selection of surveys has been provided in this article that help to indicate an athlete's susceptibility to anxiety at certain times and within certain events. The SCTAT and CSAI-2 tables provided were cited and adapted from Weinberg *et al* (2003). As an athlete completes each survey, the coach can gain an insight to the type and seriousness of an athlete's anxiety, and thus begin to apply the appropriate PST methods to address the issues.

Resource worksheets provided in this article address PST methods for effectively dealing with anxiety and over/under arousal focus on "self-talk", with additional mention to thought stopping/parking, reframing, and centring.

Part 3: Attentional Focus

Kendo World Journal, 5 (2): pp. 80-90, 2010

Overview of the topic

When athletes are asked to reflect on a good performance, many comment that they were so engrossed in the task at hand they were completely unaware of any external stimuli. Some struggle to remember the finer details of the match, where others claim that, although they were conscious of potential distractions, everything seemed to fade away as they managed to remain focused on the important job of executing the right skills at the right time. In any case, the ability to effectively focus attention to the appropriate task is commonly referred to as the feeling of "being on autopilot", and is ultimately crucial if an athlete is to execute a sequence of skills that enhance the chances of victory (Vealey, 2005; Tenenbaum & Eklund, 2007; Burton & Raedeke, 2008).

When considering the infinitesimal moment of time it takes to launch an attack in kendo, one can appreciate that even a momentary lapse in attention can lead to a devastating turn of events. Along this line of thought, the current sport psychology literature strongly advocates the important role that appropriate *attentional focus* plays in facilitating optimal performance (Williams, Nideffer, Wilson, Sagal & Peper, 2010; Vealey, 2005; Lavallee, Kremer, Moran, Williams, 2004).

This article looked at Nideffer's Attentional Model of broad-external, narrow-external, broad-internal and narrow-internal focus, in which simple labels are used in order for athletes to make sense of the psychological terms (Vealey, 2005).

- *Broad-external (big picture out there)*—allows the athlete to scan the entire environment around them and pick up the many cues in the surroundings; i.e. consider positioning in the *shiai-jō*, time left in the match and the amount of points to attempt to score.
- *Broad-internal (big picture in here)*—allows the athlete to analyse various stimuli, whilst devising a strategy based on this information; i.e. noticing the opponent drops his/her *kensen* prior to striking *men*, the athlete considers an appropriate *waza* in response is *debana-kote*.
- *Narrow-external (zoom out there)*—allows the athlete to "*zoom in*" on a target, execute a specific *waza* or react in a specific direction/way; i.e. based on the strategy to attack *debana-kote*, the athlete concentrates on the opponent's timing and the target area.
- *Narrow-internal (zoom in here)*—allows the athlete to monitor and regulate their physical and mental states, and prepare mentally to cope with the current or upcoming stressors; i.e. calming nerves, regulating arousal, breathing patterns and rehearsing focus plans and routines.

Different situations in the sporting environment will require a shift in the type of *attentional focus* the athlete should utilise. In particular, as kendo is a reactive sport, where the athlete must change his/her strategy and movements depending on the actions and reactions of the opponent (and a number of other factors), it is crucial that the kendo practitioner learns how to shift appropriately from each quadrant when required.

Resources

As the direction of an athlete's attentional focus depends on many factors, and can be altered quickly through a myriad of potential distractions come game day, the resources made available in this article address the ability to focus, re-focus, and utilise imagery.

The Focus Plan

Described as "a pre-practised plan for overcoming obstacles" (Orlick, 2008, p. 222), Burton *et al* (2008) liken the focus plan to a check-list—athletes use it to systematically run through the things they need to do at various times in a *shiai* to increase the chances of optimal performance. The focus plan is a strategy that enables the athlete to take control of the competitive event, rather than leaving distractions and upsets to chance.

Re-focus Plan

A similar skill that sets elite athletes above the rest is that of re-focusing attention when a distraction or setback is experienced (Vealey, 2005). In order to maintain peak performance throughout a day of *shiai*, the athlete must have a clear idea of their preferred responses to potential distractors and obstacles. By giving thought in advance to the many potential upsets one may face during a typical *shiai* or tournament (such as behaviour of the opponent, late arrivals to the match, perceived *shimpan* error, etc.), it is possible for the coach and athlete to devise a strategy to re-focus and move forward.

Imagery

All athletes possess images regarding themselves and their perceived abilities, and consciously or not, engage in imagery regularly (Singer *et al*, 2001; Vealey, 2005). However, the problem lays in the issue of whether the types of images or thoughts an athlete allows to dominate their minds (regarding performance) are actually productive and/or organised. In this respect, the key to successful implementation of the PST method of imagery is that it is performed systematically, and the images are controlled (Vealey, 2005; Hale, Seiser, McGuire and Weinrich, 2005). As such, this article provides an imagery "script" that the kendo coach can alter where necessary and use with his/her athlete to complement *shiai* preparation.

Part 4: Self Confidence and Goal Setting
Kendo World Journal, 5 (3): pp. 43-48, 2010

Overview of the topic

Self-confidence, or more specifically "sports confidence", is described by Vealey (1986) as the "beliefs or degree of certainty athletes possess about their ability to be successful in their sports" (p. 300). In essence, Vealey states that a healthy sense of self-confidence allows one to think productively in a variety of situations, and thus frame mistakes in a way that actually enhances further confidence and performance. In this way, a high level of self-confidence not only involves a strong belief in one's own ability to be successful, but it implies an understanding of the effort, preparation and persistence it will take to achieve success (Vealey, 2005).

Sport psychologists and coaches alike concur that acquirement of a healthy level of self-confidence is one of the most important mental skills for an athlete's success, and research continually supports the fact that confident athletes perform better than the less confident athletes in a variety of sports (Gill and Williams, 2008).

A commonly used term, "confidence" has many misconceptions surrounding it. In this regard, this article works to dispel several myths regarding self-confidence. These include:

1) Bragging shows confidence
2) An athlete must win in order to be confident
3) Successful athletes have an unshakable confidence

The ability to sustain a high level of confidence complements a number of factors necessary for ideal performance. Weinberg and Gould (1995) outline some of these as: improvements in concentration, and thus a decreased vulnerability to mental distractions; the experience of positive emotions regarding training and *shiai*, resulting in higher levels of effort; reduced muscular tension; faster and more accurate decision making skills; and an improved ability to recall game strategies (Weinberg *et al*, 1995). As such, self-confident athletes improve their chances of success right across the performance board.

However, a confident mental state is not a given for many athletes, and as such, requires the use of mental training techniques and strategies in order for it to be developed and maintained. Goal setting is commonly used for this purpose.

Resources

Goals serve to direct attention toward a particular standard that sits above the currently perceived level of skill. Sustaining the behaviour and effort required to reach these standards through *mastery* goal setting works to provide critical feedback to the athlete regarding their progress. With this feedback, athletes can more readily recognise when techniques and strategies must be altered or improved in order to achieve the task—and with every milestone reached, small or large, the athlete gradually increases his/her perception of ability and thus self-confidence.

As in previous articles, this issue also provides the coach with a practical resource in order to use it with athletes in the dojo setting. The "Goal Setting Worksheet" provided is based on resources obtained from Hodge (2004), yet has been modified slightly in areas to encourage paired work (for accountability) and includes the term "kendo" to appeal to kendo athletes as a less generic activity.

This resource concentrates on the principle of "S.M.A.R.T.S" goals, with consideration given to goal types (outcome, performance, and process) and durations (short term and long term).

Part 5: Team Cohesion and Team Goal Setting
Kendo World Journal, 5 (4): pp. 60-63, 2011

Overview of the topic

The issue of team cohesion and how best to achieve it is the topic of much sport-related literature (Brawley, Carron & Widmeyer, 1993; Martens—1987; Moran, 2004; Nakamura, 1996; Senécal, Loughead & Bloom, 2008). Cohesion is defined by Carron, Brawley, and Widmeyer (1998) as a "dynamic process that is reflected in the tendency for a group to stick together and remain united in the pursuit of its instrumental objectives and/or for the satisfaction of member affective needs" (cited in Senécal *et al.*, 2008, p. 186). Put simply, cohesive teams are able to ignore distractions in the pursuit of their common goals (Hodge, 2004) and, as research suggests, the enhancement of team cohesion relates closely to improved performance through improved team processes (Moran, 2004).

Resources

The empirical evidence covered in this article suggests that group goal setting indeed improves the cohesion of a team of people. Team goals can help motivate athletes to work more effectively together. Sports that are reliant on a high level of cooperation are more likely to benefit from team goal setting, and team-building activities, as the individuals of the team are encouraged to work together (Martens, 1987). As the team decides on a common focus, cohesion is improved and motivation to continually perform is increased (Hodge, 2004; Martens, 1987).

Over the course of this article a number of tips and considerations are highlighted regarding the best approach for a coach to take when conducting group goal setting exercises, based on recommendations from the literature. The worksheets provided in the previous article about individual goal setting (see Vol. 5.3) can also be altered slightly and used during this process.

Part 6: Aggression in Kendo I
Kendo World Journal, 6 (1): pp. 44-49, 2011

Overview of the article

Considering its historical roots in Japan's medieval combat methods, it is understandable that kendo retains a large element of intrinsic aggression. However, the instant a practitioner's control over this integral part of training is lost, harmful intents and unrestrained emotions come to the fore. It is at this point where sincere concern for the opponent's improvement, correct technique, and the goals of ethical education are left by the wayside, and the practice of kendo becomes a danger. The use, or misuse as the case may be, of various harsh training methods in kendo, such as rigorous *kakari-geiko* sessions, *kuzushi-waza,* or the employment of *mukae-zuki* may seem aggressive, violent, or even appear to resemble bullying in the eyes of some people. However, many suggest that this is not the case. A loaded issue, the need for a working definition of aggression was sought in this article.

However, as the terms "aggression" and "violence" are used to describe a reasonably wide range of behaviours, particularly in the sporting scene, much of the psychology literature regarding aggression alludes to issues surrounding the difficulty of finding a clear and agreeable definition (Kerr,

2005; Leith; 1991). As Leith points out, the word aggression can be used to negatively describe a fight between two athletes, yet at the same time, an athlete who utilises a hard body contact conducted within the rules that works to the benefit of his (or his team's) performance, can also be depicted in a positive sense as an aggressive player. In short, depending on various factors people tend to be inconsistent in their views of aggression and violence (Leith, 1991).

Part 7: Aggression in Kendo II
Kendo World Journal, 6 (2): pp. 51-58, 2012

Overview of the article
The review of the literature to this point (over Part 6 and Part 7) revealed the general principles of aggression as a noxious or harmful verbal or physical behaviour, intended to inflict physical or psychological harm or injury on an unwilling victim, with the expectancy that the behaviour will be successful. In connection, violence is an extreme form of aggressive behaviour that falls at the high end of an aggression continuum, and outside of the governing rules of the sport and laws of the land.

However, Kerr (2005) observes that many of the explanations of aggression in sport psychology literature resemble definitions offered by the parent discipline of mainstream psychology. This, he states, is problematic primarily due to the fact that although these definitions offer a general classification of the behavioural and psychological aspects of aggression, most fail to acknowledge the actions and techniques that are integral to certain sports—such as the sanctioned *kuzushi-waza* or *mukae-zuki* in kendo.

Examples of technically unsanctioned, and therefore aggressive/violent behaviour in kendo, may include foot tripping or hitting an unprotected part of the body intentionally—each of which fall outside of the written rules of a kendo competition and result in a *hansoku* (penalty). Yet interestingly, these same behaviours may be considered sanctioned and non-problematic depending on player norms within a *keiko* setting.

The idea of player norms is an important aspect of this discussion, as they allow some actions and behaviours in a kendo training (conducted outside of the competition arena, and removed from penalties and potential losses resulting from penalties) to occur within a more ambiguous realm of "acceptable" aggression. This issue emphasises the ambiguity that exists in kendo regarding contradictions between tolerable aggression in *shiai* and tolerable aggression in the dojo.

Part 8: Aggression in Kendo III
Kendo World Journal, 6 (3): pp. 65-80, 2012

Overview of the article
Without the immediate ability to determine the intent of either practitioner, one may consider how a first-time spectator of kendo is often struck by the aggressive and violent appearance of *zanshin*, *kiai*, or a fighter's general mannerisms, compounded by the display of common techniques such as *taiatari* and *tsuki*. To the outsider, kendo as a form of combat naturally reveals a fierce intensity between each practitioner as they attack each other with bamboo swords.

Despite its outwardly aggressive appearance, however, the AJKF insists that the practice of kendo encompasses and emphasises a great number of moral and ethical principles, therefore endorsing its value as a means of physical, mental and cultural education.

In accordance with the "Purpose of Practicing Kendo", the intent of the kendo practitioner should be to "hold in esteem human courtesy and honour" in order to "promote peace and prosperity" (AJKF, 1975; 2007). However in this way, a paradox exists between the ideals of modern kendo as a holistic and positive pursuit for overall human and societal development, versus the undeniable existence of aggressive approaches and misuse of the *shinai*—predominantly dictated by tradition, club customs, and player norms—by some people during harsh trainings. Therefore, as attitudes towards traditional teaching methods change, the way in which modern Japanese society interprets this paradox, and the way in which the international kendo community is expected to practise "correct Japanese kendo", become increasingly important considerations.

The objectives of kendo training and competition according to the "Concept of Kendo" (1975) and the "Mindset of Kendo Instruction" (2007) emphasise the betterment of the kendo practitioner's character. Stating terms such as "courtesy and honour", "peace and prosperity", "*kō-ken-chi-ai*" (friendship through fencing), and "a dignified and humane character", kendo practice is intended to raise a set of moralistic values that work to enhance mankind and benefit society at large. In this way, as the elements of both etiquette and safety are described as essential in the dojo, modern kendo training should be far removed from any intent to cause an opponent physical or psychological harm, because allowing aggressive behaviour directly contradicts the stated "mindset of an instructor".

According to the findings of a survey conducted into this topic (Bennett, 2010), although understanding and endeavouring to promote these ideals espoused by the AJKF, many Japanese kendo instructors, according to their individual interpretations of aggression/violence, could consider there to be a number of instances where violence is present within training (i.e. *mukae-zuki*). This in turn suggests that the full measure of care for safety and health is lacking at certain times. This is not to imply that instructors are careless in their approaches, but it raises the question as to why certain types of aggressive customs are allowed to continue, despite the obvious unethical nature of violence contradicting the purposes of kendo participation.

Part 9: Aggression in Kendo IV
Kendo World Journal, 6 (4): pp. 65-80, 2013

Overview of the article
The All Japan Kendo Federation has gone to great lengths over past decades to codify kendo rules and curb excessive aggression/violence. However, unlike the rules of kendo *shiai* that are clear and strictly upheld, there are few, if any, similar written rules that guide kendo training. As such, behaviours deemed appropriate in *keiko* tend to be limited to "unwritten rules", customs, norms and the beliefs of club members and instructors in each respective dojo. More often than not during the important process of harsh training (aimed at discipline or character development), it is this vague set of principles regarding sanctioned or unsanctioned aggression that leads to overzealousness and the misuse of *shinai*.

Although harsh training is considered an extremely effective means to instil the ideal values attainable from the practice of kendo, Japanese kendo instructors face increased societal opposition if violent misuse of the *shinai* is allowed to continue—impacting on the practice of kendo in Japan and therefore world-wide.

* * * * * * * * *

References
Psychological Skills Training articles:
- Boutcher, S.H., & Rotella, R.J. (1987). A psychological skills education program for closed-skill performance enhancement. *The Sport Psychologist*, 1, pp. 127-137.
- Brawley, L.R., Carron, A.V. & Widmeyer, W.N. (1993). The Influence of the Group and Its Cohesiveness on Perceptions of Group Goal-Related Variables. *Journal of Sport & Exercise Psychology*, 15, pp. 245-260.
- Burton, D., & Raedeke, T.D. (2008). *Sport Psychology for Coaches*. USA: Human Kinetics
- Carron, A.V., Widmeyer, W.N., & Brawley, L.R. (1985). The development of an instrument to assess cohesion in sport teams: The Group Environment Questionnaire. in J. Senécal, T.M. Loughead & G.A. Bloom, (2008). A Season-Long Team-Building Intervention: Examining the Effect of Team Building on Cohesion. *Journal of Sport & Exercise Psychology*, 30, pp. 186-199. Retrieved 10th October, 2008, from EBSCOHOST database.
- Hale, B.D., Seiser, L., McGuire, E.J. and Weinrich, E. (2005). *Mental Imagery*. In J. Taylor and G.Wilson
- (Eds.). *Applying Sport Psychology: Four Perspectives*. Champaign, Il: Human Kinetics.
- Hodge, K. (2004). *Sport Motivation; training your mind for peak performance*. Auckland: Reed Books.
- Jones, J.G., Swain, A., & Cale, A. (1990). Antecedents of multidimensional competitive state anxiety and self-confidence in elite intercollegiate middle-distance runners. *The Sport Psychologist*, 4, pp. 107-118.
- Lavallee, D., Kremer, J., Moran, A.P. and Williams, M. (2004). *Sport Psychology; Contemporary*
- *Themes*. London: Palgrave MacMilillan
- Martens, R. (1987). *Coaches guide to sport psychology*. Champaign, Il: Human Kinetics.
- Moran, A.P. (2004). *Sport and Exercise Psychology: A Critical Introduction*. London: Routledge.
- Morris, T., & Summers, J. (1995). *Sport Psychology: theory, applications and issues*. Queensland, Australia: John Wiley & Sons.
- Nakamura, R. (1996). *The Power of Positive Coaching*. London: Jones and Bartlett.
- Orlick, T. (2008). *In Pursuit Of Excellence*. 4th ed. Champaign, Il: Human Kinetics.
- Senécal, J., Loughead, T.M. & Bloom, G.A. (2008). A Season-Long Team-Building Intervention: Examining the Effect of Team Building on Cohesion. *Journal of Sport & Exercise Psychology*, 30, 186-199. Retrieved 10th October, 2008, from EBSCOHOST database.
- Singer, R.N., Hausenblas, H.A. and Janelle, C.M. (2001). *Handbook of Sport Psychology*. 2nd ed. New
- York, NY: Wiley & Sons, Inc.
- Tenenbaum, G. and Eklund, R.C. (2007). *Handbook of Sport Psychology*. 3rd ed. New Jersey: John
- Wiley & Sons, Inc.
- Vealey, R.S. (1986). Conceptualization of sport-confidence and competitive orientation: Preliminary investigation and instrument development. *Journal of Sport Psychology*, 8, pp. 221-246.
- Vealey, R.S. (2005). *Coaching for the Inner Edge*. USA: Fitness Information Technology.
- Visek, A.J., Harris, B.S., & Blom, L.C. (2009). Doing sport psychology: A youth sport consulting model for practitioners. *The Sport Psychologist*, 23, pp. 271-291.
- Weinberg, R.S., & Gould, D. (1995). *Foundations of sport & exercise psychology*. Champaign, IL: Human Kinetics.
- Weinberg, R.S., & Gould, D. (2003). *Foundations of Sport & Exercise Psychology*. 3rd ed. USA: Human
- Kinetics.
- Williams, J.M., Nideffer, R.M., Wilson, V.E., Sagal, M. and Peper, E. (2010). *Concentration and Strategies for Controlling It*. In J.M. Williams (Ed.), *Applied Sport Psychology; Personal Growth to Peak Performance*. 6th ed. New York, NY: McGraw-Hill.

Aggression articles:
- All Japan Kendo Federation (1975). *The Concept of Kendo*. Retrieved July 1, 2010, from http://www.kendo-fik.org/english-page/english-page2/concept-of-Kendo.htm
- All Japan Kendo Federation (2007). *The Mind-set of Kendo Instruction(剣道指導の心構え)*. Retrieved July 1, 2010, from http://www.kendo-fik.org/english-page/english-page2/concept-of-Kendo.htm
- All Japan Kendo Federation (Ed.). (2000). Japanese-English Dictionary of Kendo (2nd ed.). Tokyo: Satou Insho-kan.
- Bennett, B. (2010). *Towards an Understanding of Aggression and Violence in School Kendo Training; the issues facing current kendo instruction methods* (Master's Thesis). Osaka University of Health and Sport Science Library.
- Kerr, J.H. (1997). *Motivation and emotion in sport: reversal theory*. East Essex, UK: Taylor & Francis Group.
- Kerr, J.H. (2005). *Rethinking aggression and violence in sport*. New York, NY: Routledge.
- Leith, L. (1991). Aggression. In S.J. Bull (Ed.), *Sport psychology: a self-help guide* (pp.52-69). Ramsbury, Marlborough: The Crowood Press Ltd.

Tachikiri

By Jonathan Levine-Ogura

The *taiko* drum signals the end of the last match with its deep spiritual Shintō resonance. The atmosphere feels as if all the *motodachi* crossed the finish line in a photo finish. They are barely standing, but their spirit is unbroken. A final *sonkyo* along with the 33rd *kakarite*, euphemistically called *chōsensha* (challenger), is performed, but the *motodachi* is barely up to it. It has previously been done 32 times at five minute intervals, starting three hours before. Then, standing once again with a firm "*Shōmen ni, rei*" from the chief referees, a final bow is performed, and the arena breaks into delicate celebration. All the *chōsensha* rush to their respective courts and wait while the *motodachi*, almost ceremoniously upon the *tatami*, remove their *men* as if they were the only ones left standing on the battlefield. The *motodachi* is given a *dō-age* (a toss high into the air) three times by the *chōsensha*; handshakes, sweat and tears soon follow. A living kendo legend is born and so ends this year's *tachikiri-jiai* (立切試合), an epic and heroic moment for all to see.

Every mid-January, when streets of snow canyons form in the hot spring city of Yuzawa, Akita Prefecture, in northern Japan, four male and two female competitors called *motodachi* compete in an event called *tachikiri-jiai*. Possessing superb physical skills and mental strength developed over years of disciplined training, they had been chosen by a committee of high-ranking kendoka from the previous year to participate in a marathon *shiai* event, lasting three hours for men and two for women.

As this competition should not be taken lightly, a full year of physical and psychological training, along with years of regular *keiko*, is necessary for successful completion, or in Japanese, "*tachikiru*", as the competition name suggests. For a successful outcome, the *motodachi* should stay standing (*tachi*—立ち), both "physically" and "mentally", while following through with complete effort (*kiru*—切る—a highly nuanced word that does not only mean "cut"). It is perhaps a perfect example of budo philosophy and sport being fused into a single event. In other words, the *motodachi*, who are generally 6-dan and above, must have the physical stamina and great mental fortitude to overcome each new successive *chōsensha* in competition format, who are selected from a group of volunteers, and discover a path toward kendo enlightenment. Getting "into the zone" would be the most applicable way describe it. The process of this type of *keiko* should take the *motodachi* to a higher level of kendo in the allotted period of time.

The format is quite simple, but here lies the dilemma the *motodachi* faces. They face off against 33 *chōsensha* in a *shiai* with unlimited scoring, not *sanbon-shōbu*, in five minute bouts for three hours. The women face off against 22 female *chōsensha*, starting one hour later for a two hour competition that runs parallel to the men's. In a normal *shiai*, participants wear red and white *tasuki*, but in a *tachikiri*, the *motodachi* always wears an extra-long white high-quality cotton *mejirushi*. His or her name and *dan* are written in beautiful calligraphy to signify their special place on the court. The *chōsensha* are always red. *Shimpan* are assigned to each court with the usual strict and orderly rotation, and judge matches in accordance

with the All Japan Kendo Federation (AJKF) *shiai* rules. Interestingly, the chief referees must face *shōmen* so the left side court flags are reversed because the *motodachi*'s position is always white. In other words, the *motodachi* have the centre position in the arena while the *chōsensha* enter from the sides.

Is it *shiai* or *ji-geiko*, or a combination of both? The *motodachi* must reconcile this incongruity both physically and mentally in order to reach their thirty-third opponent three hours later. An *ippon* is still an *ippon*, whether you are against your first or last opponent. A successful *motodachi* who has reconciled this issue will be at ease. They will eventually see openings under great pressure from a fresh *chōsensha*, even after countless attacks over the three hour period. Physically exhausted, they have crossed the threshold to mental acuity. In the end, physical strength is actually a weakness, and it can never be relied upon while being the *motodachi*. Hard to believe, but it has happened to each and every *motodachi* that I have spoken to. The results are more wins than losses or draws, and high winning percentages are always the norm. It is a superhuman accomplishment.

The atmosphere is almost carnival-like; something akin to a coming-of-age ceremony would be the best way to explain it. Akita Prefecture is known for its rich *sake* and drinking customs, and this is actually a weekend event Akita style. Beginning Saturday afternoon, an open *keiko-kai* is held with many 8-dan sensei in attendance, some coming from as far away as Osaka. In the evening there is a reception for the *motodachi* and all the *chōsensha* at Yuzawa's top hotel. Since this is a celebratory event for the *motodachi*, there is a ridiculous amount of drinking and bar hopping afterwards. The next morning the competition begins shortly after 10:00 and the smell of alcohol lingers in the air. The theme song to Rocky is played when the *motodachi* enter! Among the *chōsensha*, a sense of camaraderie is quite evident with *ji-geiko* beforehand and a group warm-up to bring everyone together.

Large banners with messages of support and good luck, including *senba-zuru* (1000 folded cranes) are hung on the arena walls by sempai, kohai, students, co-workers, and family members for their respective *motodachi*. There is a small team of close supporters who are allowed to help the *motodachi* at specific intervals between matches to give water and some assistance. Too much help is frowned upon, however. Again, they were chosen for their skills and worthy kendo character and it is assumed they will complete the event with fortitude and grace.

The history of the *tachikiri-jiai* goes back to the Edo Period. In order to become a great kenshi, a vow was taken by young pupils upon entering a fencing school. In that vow they were expected to complete long training sessions in order to acquire the highest level of swordsmanship. Training was done in three terms and direct approval and instruction from the dojo master himself was necessary to begin. There would be no days of rest whatsoever.

The first term was the so-called *shōtōka* (elementary training course) and was cumulative training over a three year time span. On the last day of the third year, the pupil endured a *tachikiri* session of 200 bouts. Successful pupils would then graduate and move to the second term called *futsūka* (general training course), which would last many years depending on the pupil's progress. After many sessions of accumulated training the pupil would then again endure a *tachikiri* session lasting three days of 600 bouts. After graduating from the general training course the pupil would finally enter the *kōtōka* (advanced course) and endure brutal training in order to complete the final *tachikiri* session of 1400 *shiai* over a seven-day period. With this final superhuman feat accomplished, the pupil would finally be christened and granted the noble rank of kenshi from this school of swordsmanship.

Those who could obtain this level were far from many and it took a special person to complete the course. It is said that after many successive bouts, under extreme conditions, the *tachikiri motodachi* were able to endure any environment without fear or innocence of battle. These *motodachi* perhaps acquired a great sense of situational awareness to overcome any adversary including himself, the weakest link.

Which brings me back to the modern form of Yuzawa's *tachikiri*. The theory and premise behind the event is essentially the same except that it is done in a controlled environment under the strict rules and auspices of the AJKF. It is always done in winter to prevent dehydration. (Iwate Prefecture's own *tachikiri* in Tono City was moved to later in the year out of concern for the *motodachi* succumbing to dehydration.) After watching many *tachikiri* and being a *chōsensha* myself, I have been in awe of the *motodachi* enduring successive bouts and not withering to the competition. Each *chōsensha* faces all *motodachi* in rotating 11-member teams to compete three times. Women *chōsensha* face the two female *motodachi* to compete two times. In my 16 years of watching this event I have only seen two male *motodachi* fail to finish, and that was due to dehydration and a ruptured Achilles tendon. All female competitors have always completed the event by winning almost all of their 22 bouts over a 14-year period with an average winning percentage of 75 per cent. Over a 34-year period the men have been averaging at 75 per cent as well. The *motodachi* who has the most wins is declared the winner of the event. Consolation prizes are given to second place and a single third place as well, so the pressure to perform well certainly exists which adds to the drama and ultimate paradox of kendo's rigid dichotomy between sport and budo philosophy.

As of now there have been 128 male *motodachi* participants. The *motodachi* with the best results stands at 31 wins, zero losses and two draws resulting in a 96.9 winning percentage set more than 26 years ago, and that *motodachi* is now a 8-dan. Four years ago it was equalled, but there has never been a *motodachi* that has beaten all 33 *chōsensha*. In the female division there have been 13 competitions with 22 *motodachi* participating. The female record currently stands at 20 wins, zero losses and two draws with a 95.5 winning percentage.

Chōsensha are also awarded prizes for the most wins against the *motodachi*. A *chōsensha* is awarded one point for one win and a half point for a draw. If there is a tie in winning percentage among *chōsensha*, the one with the most wins is awarded the prize. If the numbers of wins are the same then the *chōsensha* with the most points taken from the *motodachi* is declared the final winner. Out of the 33 *chōsensha*, they are naturally the strongest and are usually chosen to be next year's *motodachi*.

To my knowledge, this is one of the few remaining *tachikiri* events left in northern Japan while many other *tachikiri-jiai* have disappeared. In the neighbouring prefecture of Iwate, the final *tachikiri-jiai* took place this year ending 30 years of a tradition in Tono City. Whether it will be revived in another city is up for consideration. However, with a lack of young participants due to a shrinking and aging population it has become harder to find willing *motodachi* and *chōsensha* to make an event like this a success.

As I recall at the pre-event hotel reception from this year's *tachikiri* the organisers were proud to say in their speeches how this event has never seen any loss in participants and enthusiasm. It has become an annual event and a winter tradition for Yuzawa. This not only represents the status of strong kendo in the Yuzawa area, but for Akita Prefecture in general. I believe with this event they have managed to grapple the paradox of budo and sport and bring back, or rather sustain, the true spirit of *keiko* in today's modern kendo world.

The *shiai* is free to attend and all pre- and post-*keiko* events are open to join. For a mid-January kendo trip to Japan, this is an excellent opportunity to experience the snowy rural north with hot springs and good country food and drink to warm up to after *keiko*. I truly believe this should be on anyone's kendo bucket list. Why not come along and experience something different?

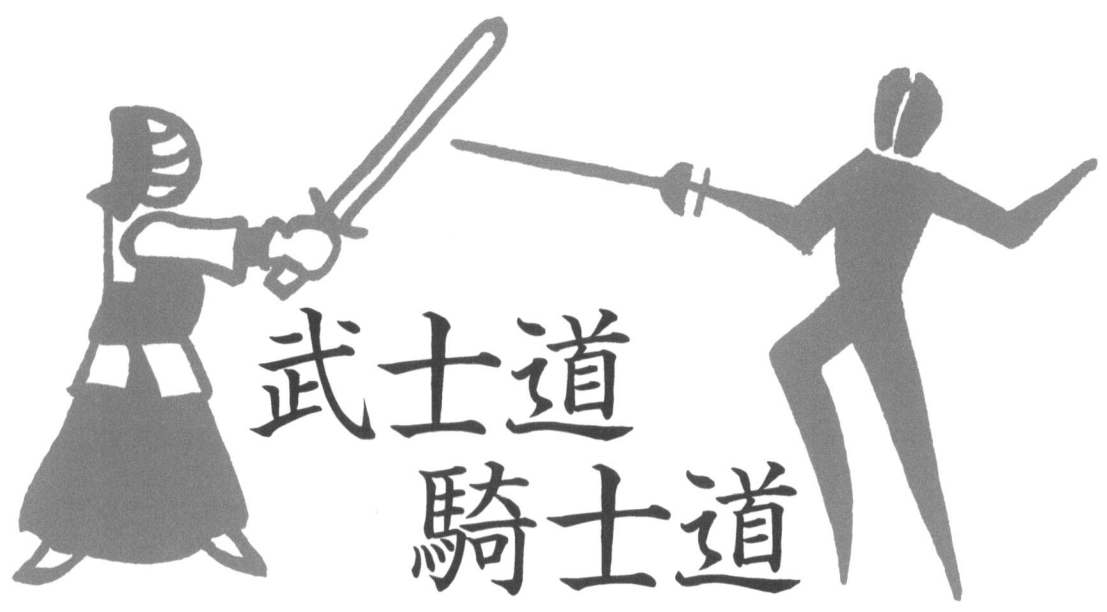

A Comparative Analysis of Bushido and Chivalry
Part Two

By Ryan McIntyre

What bushido and chivalry have most in common is that they are both fraught with misconception. Emerging as geographically distant, though philosophically similar equivalents, they were not static moral codes; rather, they were, and potentially still are, multifaceted, complicated and constantly changing social phenomena. Part two of this essay will continue to attempt to trace the chronological origins of bushido and chivalry, identify and compare their core philosophies, investigate their development throughout history, and discuss the influence of these two systems on both medieval and modern society.

DEVELOPMENT AND INFLUENCE ON SOCIETY

Both chivalry and bushido show a trend of significant development during times of peace, as a purely military code no longer had relevance within peaceful society.[1] During the late twelfth century, significant developments in theology and philosophy formed the background for the growth of chivalry. Early medieval literature stressed the helplessness of humans in the face of a terrifying and unforgiving God. However, this school of thought was gradually replaced with positive notions concerning rationality, human agency and the intellectual accessibility of the universe.[2] God was humanised, and the Virgin Mary became a role model for women of all classes. The knight of this time period, influenced by the changing social and intellectual atmosphere, became an idealised figure.

> "Influenced by the twelfth-century cultural awakening, the culture of chivalry was richer, subtler and more diverse than the culture of earlier centuries. It complemented heroism with a range of literary and artistic references that invested it with an emotional intensity which in an earlier age would have been inconceivable."[3]

The new image of the knight was accompanied by an increasingly idealised version of chivalry in literature: "the chivalric lifestyle of the aristocracy found its mirror in literature, just as literature found much of its inspiration

---

1 Stevenson, p .2; Ikegami, p. 278
2 Saul, p. 38
3 Ibid

in chivalry."[4] Romantic narrative grew immensely popular, and detailed what was considered to be chivalric, especially the courtly treatment of women, but this literature does not necessarily reflect the reality of the time. As this literature became more idealised, so too did the image of chivalry,[5] "indicative of the best virtues of manhood one could attain."[6] In a similar fashion, an idealisation of the samurai occurred, though it was not through the popularity of literature, but rather the social requirements of a Confucian hierarchy system.

While neo-Confucianism was the official code of ethical direction for the shogunate, and Zen Buddhism was the religion the warrior class tended to be most involved in, bushido itself came to be a pseudo-religion in its own right. As the samurai continued to search for their role in peace times, they "internalized the Confucian virtues and served as a sort or moral exemplar for the farmer, artisan and merchant."[7]

Nitobe supports this concept, suggesting that "though [the samurai] kept themselves socially aloof from the populace, they set a moral standard for them and guided them by their example... the precepts of [bushido] began at first as the glory of the elite, but became in time an aspiration and inspiration to the nation at large."[8] Essentially, samurai became "living examples of dedication to one's duty."

Chivalry also had a remarkable effect on the development of well-defined laws of war conduct, which became universal across Europe by the fifteenth century. Due to the great effectiveness, and great cost of cavalry, the majority of those who waged war were wealthy nobles. The aristocracy who participated in war were, by the fifteenth century, expected to obey these chivalric laws of combat.[9] Also during the mid-fifteenth century, "a new model of the ideal knight emerged."[10] Emphasis shifted from warrior values to administrative roles, and knights became far more assimilated into courtly life than before. Many knights sought honour and reputation as lawyers, writers and translators of military strategy and chivalry, though the popularity of tournaments ensured that martial prowess was not entirely forgotten.[11]

Tournaments became an important part of peace time chivalry. These events provided an arena for knights to develop martial prowess and gain fame; they could practise their techniques in non-lethal combat scenarios and also win social renown.[12] Success in tournaments earned the victors fame and money, and even in peace times lower landless knights became distinguished. Ironically, for many knights martial skill came to hold more importance during peace times than war.[13] The division between lesser, landless knights and landed nobility began to blur, and the more obvious distinction was between those who were knights, and those who were not, as the knights began to merge into a single elite class.[14] While it was perhaps not overly common (as tournaments tended to be primarily public entertainment), there are accounts of tournaments developing into more serious affairs with the intention of teaching younger participants the realities of war. Knights could be captured and ransomed within the tournament, and the captor was able to claim his victim's armour as a legitimate spoil of war.[15] These tournaments were initiated at the request of churchmen eager to stop lawless battles that broke out between restless knights by providing a physical outlet for warriors that was both non-lethal and within the law.[16]

The *kenka ryōseibai* law of the Tokugawa period was introduced for a similar reason; it was a law that sought to prevent unsanctioned, personal feuds from escalating and undermining the authority of the shogunate. During pax Tokugawa, as Ikegami points out, the medieval violent notion of honour was no longer taken for granted as acceptable behaviour in society. The samurai were less associated with violence and more with virtuous self-discipline.

Similarly, in the sixteenth century, violence and aggression came to be seen as an unsophisticated lack of restraint across Europe, a far cry from the knightly ideal of only a few hundred years before.[17] Within samurai society, the martial arts fulfilled essentially the same function as European knightly tournaments; the martial arts gave the warrior class a means to temper their martial skills, as well as eventually test them against others in non-lethal combat. Even in peace time samurai continued to receive stipends from their lords, so it was their duty to remain vigilant and battle-ready. With the invention of safe training equipment such as protective armour and bamboo swords (*shinai*) in the 1700s, samurai were able to engage in a sportified version of *kenjutsu*. The participants not only tested their abilities, but had the opportunity to win fame, and even money.

Another especially important development in bushido in the sixteenth and seventeenth centuries was the samurai's

---

4 Ibid, p. 37
5 Stevenson, p. 131
6 Milby, p. 14
7 Hurst, p. 521
8 Nitobe, p. 48
9 Strickland, p. 31
10 Stevenson, p. 39
11 Ibid.

12 Saul, p. 17
13 Ibid
14 Strickland, p. 22
15 Saul, p. 17
16 Ibid., p. 16
17 Stevenson, p. 40

diminishing willingness to die for their lord. While some lamented the decline of *seppuku*, once considered an honourable and even exemplary death, it came to be considered a relic of a bygone and overly violent era.[18]

Junshi, committing *seppuku* to follow one's lord into the afterlife in the ultimate display of affection and loyalty, was eventually banned in the Tokugawa era to prevent unnecessary deaths, though it was by that time not overly common anyway due to the samurai's changing attitudes towards death.[19] In the Tokugawa era, *seppuku* even came to be used as a form of punishment.[20] While lower class criminals tended to simply be beheaded, samurai were often afforded the opportunity to commit *seppuku*. While there were still instances of samurai committing *seppuku* in the name of honour, it had become a punishment, reserved for the nobility, but a punishment nonetheless. The samurai who died in this way did not do so out of any wilful act of loyalty or demonstration of moral principle, but to atone for their sins.[21]

While martial codes will inevitably lose relevance in peace time, in Europe this was hastened by the ever-shrinking social gap between the warrior elite and merchant classes. Chivalry "binded knights and nobles to a common philosophy",[22] and grew in reputation because of its growing administrative proximity to the monarch.[23] However, the military elite's martial prowess had lost much of its significance, and the initial status marker of wealth was quickly fading; knightly reputation alone soon came to be the sole distinguishing factor of the warrior class.[24] Similarly, the Meiji Restoration not only abolished the feudal system in 1868, but consequently forbade samurai their ancient privileges of carrying swords and wearing the warrior topknot in 1876. This monumental event in many ways signalled the end of the samurai. In 1869, the samurai's hierarchical status was demoted to *shizoku*, "descendants of samurai", whose legal rights were subsequently abolished in 1882.

Both chivalry and bushido had considerable impact on their respective societies for hundreds of years. They both developed significantly in a variety of ways. One of the most distinctive, though surprisingly common elements of both bushido and chivalry was, and possibly is, their ability to adapt: while these codes greatly influenced society, they in turn also had to evolve to retain their relevance within that society. This, of course, raises the question of whether bushido and chivalry still remain today.

---

18 Hurst, p. 520
19 Ibid.
20 Ibid., p. 522
21 Ibid.
22 Stevenson, p. 6
23 Rodriguez-Velasco, p. 17
24 Stevenson, pp. 9-10

MODERN DAY RELEVANCE

A question that is often asked of bushido and chivalry is, do they still exist today? While Nitobe Inazo would suggest or hope otherwise, the cynical (though not entirely inaccurate) answer is "no". Even bushido and chivalry of the sixteenth century were far removed from their twelfth century counterparts; the periods of peace in Europe and Japan promoted unprecedented development within their respective warrior codes. Bushido and chivalry, as idealised moral systems guiding an elite warrior class, still influence various facets of life today, including moral ideals video games, movies and other popular media; however, as actual legitimate behavioural codes, they are not so visible. If chivalry and bushido do indeed still exist today, then they do so as only a faint shadow of their original forms, that is, complex mixtures of martial, political, spiritual and philosophical elements. Bushido and chivalry no longer exist in such a complicated shape because they no longer need to, and would not have enough relevance within modern society to sustain their existence today. Nitobe suggests that "in manifold ways has bushido filtered down from the social class where it originated . . . furnishing a moral standard for the whole people."[25] His use of the word "filtered" in one sense could imply a refinement of bushido, though interestingly at the same time indicates that much of the essence of bushido has been filtered out and lost, strained away over centuries of change.

In pre-World War II Japan, the *Hagakure* and Nitobe Inazo's *Bushido* were given much hype by the militaristic government. The wartime interpretation of bushido was essentially ultra-nationalistic and militaristic war propaganda,[26] and arguably had little in common with the messages of the texts they used as an educational foundation, other than twisted messages for subjugation and sacrifice. The martial arts, once a core facet of bushido, also came to be used in a similar way, teaching children militaristic patriotism disguised as spiritual development. While the military teachings of World War II Japan seem on the surface to be reminiscent of their bushido influence, in critical retrospect, this 'bushido' was only tenuously connected with the code that supposedly inspired it. Similarly, it often boasted in Japan that the typical Japanese salary worker's unflinching 'loyalty' to their company is clearly visible evidence of modern bushido. However, the modern Japanese company system, where workers are rewarded not on their individual ability but rather how long they have remained within the company, was established in 1910 precisely because of disloyalty. Previously, Japanese workers had frequently changed jobs to suit their own economic

---

25 Nitobe, p. 48
26 Hurst, p. 511

interests (as samurai had previously changed masters),[27] and the new system was designed to bind employees to a single company.[28] While Japanese business is often said to reflect numerous qualities of bushido, the very nature of these two concepts is contradictory: bushido, and the Confucian ideals that so strongly influenced it, encouraged detachment from the material world, especially such base pursuits as business and money making (perhaps explaining why the merchant class was despised in the early-modern).[29]

The belief that the virtues encouraged through chivalry are still applicable today is also not uncommon.[30] The idea of an internal moral compass is appealing, though many of these concepts, such as objective justice, simply cannot work within the framework of today's post-modern and morally ambiguous society. While Nitobe was of course discussing Japan of the late 1800s and early 1900s, he believed that bushido was the innate guiding moral force of the entirety of the Japanese people:

> … deep rooted and powerful is still the effect of Bushido . . . it is an unconscious and mute influence. The heart of the people responds, without knowing why, to any appeal made to what it has inherited.[31] . . . Bushido as an independent code of ethics may vanish, but its power will not perish from the earth; its schools of martial prowess or civil honor may be demolished, but its light and glory will long survive their ruins. Like its symbolic flower, after it is blown to the four winds, it will still bless mankind with the perfume with which it will enrich life.[32]

Nitobe himself realises that the martial and civil elements, essentially two-thirds of what comprised bushido in the first place, are gone. Does the "power" of bushido still subtly direct the Japanese people, or is Nitobe and his throngs of followers today simply attaching the name of an ancient warrior code onto expected social behaviour? Furthermore, saying that bushido is an intrinsic part of all Japanese people is as inaccurate as saying that chivalry is inherent in all European people. The fact that it sounds more plausible, however, is evidence of how far reaching Nitobe's work was.

CLOSING THOUGHTS

It is optimistic, though perhaps not entirely academic, to believe that bushido and chivalry are still alive. Naturally, notions of courtesy, loyalty, generosity, honesty, decent behaviour, and perhaps even heroic individuals, still exist today, though this is not necessarily evidence of the unconscious influence of, or an active dedication to, bushido or chivalry. Perhaps some historians, and undeniably modern media, have anachronistically attached more significance to the followers of bushido and chivalry as behavioural paragons than whatever actually existed. Nitobe's book "Bushido: The Soul of Japan" caused enormous excitement, and sparked a boom of interest in Japanese culture. Basil Hall Chamberlain, a contemporary of Nitobe, aptly suggested that the unexpected popularity of Nitobe's work was essentially "the founding of a new religion."[33] Of course, it is entirely possible that bushido existed more as a didactic model of excellence than a strict code. Chivalry also was perhaps not so much a guide to social etiquette as an ideal for knights to aspire to.[34] While both chivalry and bushido presented warriors with a noble objective, both knights and samurai were, while surely ambitious and highly influential in their time, ultimately human. It is almost unthinkable by today's standards to envision ordinary men, warrior or not, reaching the heights of physical and spiritual perfection promoted by bushido and chivalry. As Nitobe himself agrees, "few ethical systems are better entitled to the rank of religion than bushido."[35] This idea applies to both bushido and chivalry; both have been embellished and idealised so much over centuries of intellectual and romantic reflection that they are at the very least deserving of the title of legend.

References:

- Archer, Joshua. "Understanding Samurai Disloyalty" in *New Voices V.2* (date?) pp.80-102.
- Durlabhji, Subhash, Norton E. Marks. "Introduction" in *Japanese Business: Cultural Perspectives* (Subhash Durlabhji and Norton E. Marks Eds.) Albany: State University of New York Press, 1993.
- Ikegami, Eiko. *The Taming of the Samurai: Honorific Individualism and the Making of Modern Japan*. Cambridge, Mass: Harvard University Press, 1995.
- Hurst III, Cameron G.. "Death, honour and Loyalty: The Bushido Ideal" in *Philosophy East and West, V.40 No. 4* (October 1990). pp.511-527. University of Hawaii Press.
- Milby, Gary. *The Chivalrous Man: Chivalry and the Godly Man*. Enumclaw: WinePress Publishing, 2006.
- Nitobe, Inazo. *Bushido: The Soul of Japan*. 1908. Gutenberg Project eBook 2004. (http://fliiby.com/file/213604/x1auzb5f68.html)
- Rodriguez-Velasco, Jesus D.. *Order and Chivalry: Knighthood and Citizenship in Late Medieval Castile*. Eunice Rodriguez Ferguson trans. Pennsylvania: University of Philadelphia Press, 2010.
- Saul, Nigel. *Chivalry in Medieval England*. Cambridge: First Harvard University Press, 2011.
- Stevenson, Katie. *Chivalry and Knighthood in Scotland 1424-1513*. Woodbridge: The Boydell Press, 2006.
- Strickland, Matthew. *War and Chivalry: The Conduct and Perception of War in England and Normandy, 1066-1217*. Cambridge: Cambridge University Press, 1996.

---

27 Archer, p. 81
28 Hurst, p. 517
29 Durlabhji, p. 17
30 Milby, p. 17
31 Nitobe, p. 52
32 Ibid., p. 55

33 Hurst, p. 513
34 Stevenson, p. 3
35 Nitobe, p. 48

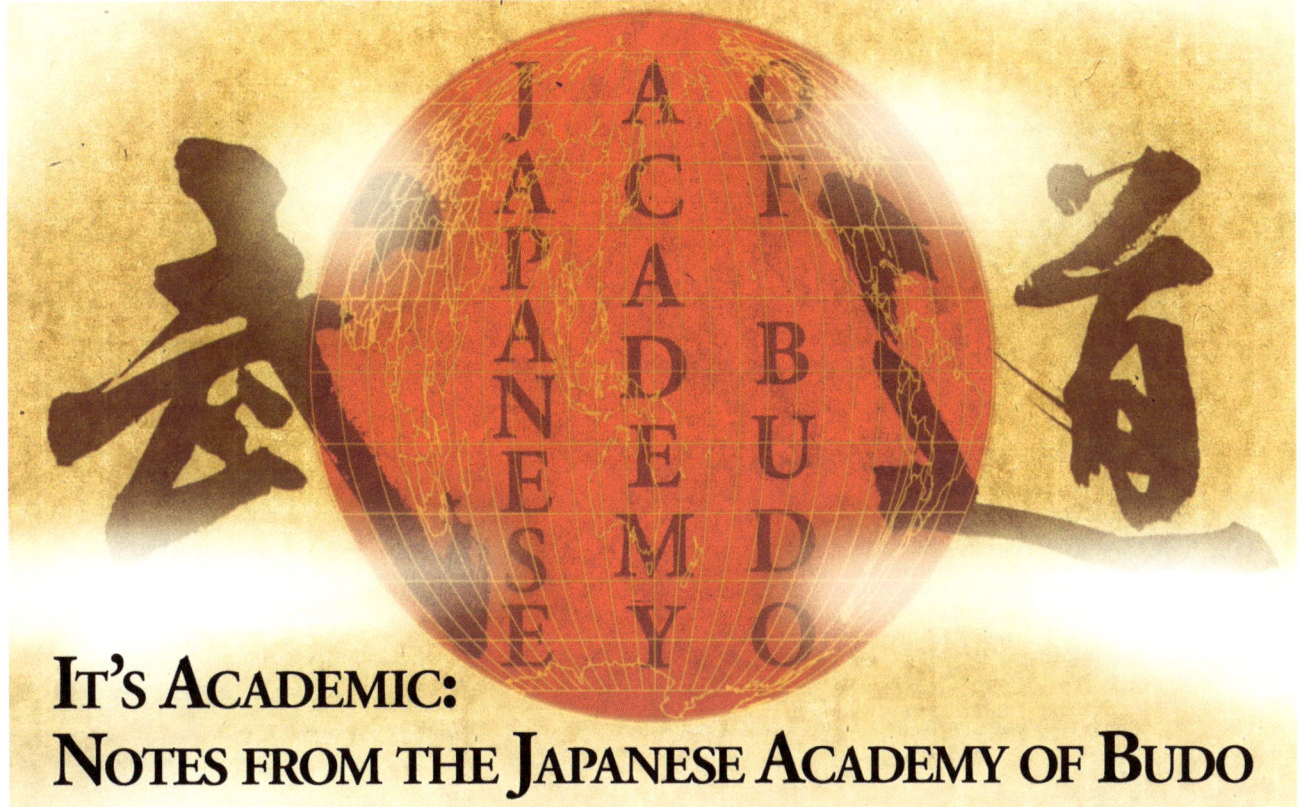

It's Academic:
Notes from the Japanese Academy of Budo

In the 1960s, many scholars recognised there was a need for sound academic analysis of the technical, historical, cultural and social aspects of budo. The Nippon Budokan led a movement to create an elite academic society dedicated to budo research. The Japanese Academy of Budo was officially launched on December 25, 1967. Each year, members congregate for the annual convention to present and discuss all aspects of budo culture. The 2013 International Budo Conference was held at the University of Tsukuba. The event marked the 141st year since the founding of the Tokyo Higher Normal School, the predecessor to the University of Tsukuba. Its name has changed from Tokyo Higher Normal School to Tokyo Liberal Arts and Science University, then to Tokyo University of Education, and finally to the University of Tsukuba. The University of Tsukuba also celebrated its 40th anniversary in 2013. This university has been at the forefront of budo research, especially in the post-war period. Actually, the first president of the school was Kanō Jigorō, the founder of judo.

The 2013 conference received support from the Nippon Budokan Foundation, and was able to be convened through cooperation from academic societies such as the International Martial Arts and Combat Sports Scientific Society, the Korean Alliance of Martial Arts, the Forum for Budo Culture, and the International Association of Judo Researchers. This marked the first time that the society's annual conference was held with a special international session. The international sessions resulted in meaningful and stimulating dialogue on budo, including a symposium titled "Integrated Science of Budo". This symposium sought to elucidate how budo, as a competitive pursuit, is also highly valued culturally and is spreading throughout the world.

The following list of presentations/papers is from the convention's proceedings. The papers have all been translated into English, and will be a valuable contribution to the future direction of international budo research.

2013, Sep. 10 (Tues.)

1 B-3: Changes in the condition of the elite athlete: In view of the World Judo Championships before and after 2011

1 I-1: Lost in translation?: The challenges of rendering Miyamoto Musashi into English

1 I-4: An investigation of the intended learning outcomes of Japanese high school physical education teachers: A comparison of kendo and rugby instructors

1 I-5: The current situation of judo in Germany: An analysis of the teaching and training program of the German Judo Federation

1 I-6: Effects of the International Judo Federation referee rules on competition contents in the All Japan Judo Championships: A 2008–2013 comparison

1 I-7: The consciousness analysis of teachers teaching

required martial arts in physical education in Japan: Male and female physical education teachers teaching judo at the junior high school level

1 I-8: Factor analytic study on the psychology of judo: In the case of judo *kata* athletes

1 I-9: A pattern of disseminating jujutsu and judo overseas before World War II: An analysis of *"JUDO: Forty-one Lessons in the Modern Science of Jiu-Jitsu"*

Sep. 11 (Wed.)

II B-5: A consideration about *monouchi*

II B-9: Side-to-side differences of calcaneal bone mass in kendo players

II C-2: A consideration of the use of the *shinai* for the instruction of beginners: Focusing on the measurement of striking force

II I-1: Information dynamics in judo

II I-2: A study of the typical mistakes in Koshiki No Kata and their correction

II I-3: Leg extension power in heavyweight elite judo athletes

II I-4: Motion analysis of standing techniques in women's judo

II I-5: Dialogue regarding intrinsic challenges for karatedo teaching and practice: multidimensional training variables and factors from exercise to macrocycles planning

II I-7: The reception of G. Funakoshi's philosophy in traditional karate (ITKF) circle in the Lublin region

II I-8: A study of the founding of dojo by female karate instructors and their teaching activities

II I-9: Kinesiological analysis of karate front kick on Portuguese elite competitors in comparison with black belt non-competitive practitioners

II I-10: Mechanics of an arrow

II P-1: The formation of the warrior's status through physical techniques in the early modern period: Based on a review of the Yamaga-ryū Heihō Series

II P-2: An electromyographic study of the lower limb muscles during *fumikomi* movement in kendo and karate athletes

II P-3: Expertise differences in *maai* maneuvers in kendo matches

II P-4: Quantitative characterization of the kendo *men* strike from electromyography and kinesiology

II P-6: Improvement of flow state during practice of *kyudo* through autogenic training

Sept. 12 (Thur.)

III A-1: Clarifying the medical culture "*kappō*" by considering the techniques (mind and body) of martial arts at the basis of the *judo-kappō*

III B-1: The exercise intensity of *osoto-gari uchikomi* in male university judokas

III B-7: The final posture of *ukemi* (the falling method) analyzed by Information Entropy

III B-9: Translational and rotational head acceleration in judo throwing techniques

III B-11: A study of motion in *seoi-nage* in different methods of *kumite* done by lightweight women judo players

III C-8: Consideration for a new judgement system for kendo matches: A trial to bring out the best in kendo

III I-2: The "re-civilising" process of kendo in the immediate post-war period: An analysis of the significance of *shinai-kyōgi*

III I-3: Research on the worth of kendo associated with its internationalization: Comparison of Korean kumdo and Japanese kendo

III I-4: Wartime *naginata* education: a survey of the Monbushō Seitei Kata

III I-5: Japanese postures toward the international development of *naginata*: A study from the 1960s to the present day

III I-6: Budo practice as a means for post-stroke rehabilitation: Case studies

III I-7: Ulysses S. Grant and the display of martial arts in the Meiji era: From "*jutsu* (technique)" to "culture"

III I-8: The differences between Jujutsu and Judo: Modifications to Jujutsu made by Jigorō Kanō in creating Judo

III P-1: The effects of an exercise program applied with Gōjū-ryū karatedo *kata* breathing methods on physical and mental aspects in elderly women

III P-2: A functional MR imaging trial for kata motor imagery tasks of experts in karate and judo

III P-3: Physical safety and mental benefits of exercise prescription based on Gōjū-ryū karatedo kata breathing method for Japanese elderly

III P-4: Motion analysis of the stand technique for men in the All Japan Judo Championship

III P-5: The pushing or pulling force exertion under unbalanced conditions

III P-6: Risk assessment of *Staphylococcus aureus* in judo athletes

III P-8: Investigation into the actual situation of boys' judo instruction in Japan

Electromyographic Patterns during Kendo *Hiki-waza* Strikes in Kendoka of Different Experience

By Yotani K., Maesaka S.
National Institute of Fitness and Sports in Kanoya, JAPAN

Abstract

Muscle activity patterns in the arms during *hiki-waza* were assessed using electromyographic (EMG) analysis. Fourteen males (seven kendo athletes [kendoka] group; seven non-kendoka) were asked to perform a strike in response to visual stimulation from a flashing light signal. The strikes, *hiki-men* (men) and *hiki-kote* (kote), were performed as quickly as possible with a *shinai* using the arms. EMG signals from the bilateral biceps brachii, bilateral triceps brachii and the right flexor carpi ulnaris muscles were recorded together with elbow joint angle and striking force. The kendoka group altered the timing of the recruitment of muscles in accordance with the different striking tasks, i.e., *men* and *kote*. The non-kendoka group altered the EMG magnitude in accordance with the different striking tasks. These results suggest that there is a difference in neuromuscular function for *men* and *kote* tasks between experienced and inexperienced kendoka groups.

Keywords: Electromyogram, muscle activity pattern, *hiki-waza*

I. Introduction

Ki-ken-tai-itchi is emphasised in kendo, but even though physical strength is important, one of kendo's main points is nerve-muscle training. (Ono et al., 1968; 1969) Furthermore, in a kendo match the *shinai* must be manipulated with both hands at any given moment and depending on the actions of the opponent, in order to quickly score a *yūkō-datotsu* (valid strike). In that way, striking in kendo is similar to baseball or golf, not in that the body is made to rotate working together with a tool (i.e. a bat or club), but that the left and right arms have contrasting movements (right pushes; left pulls) to make the *shinai* rotate. Skills that principally involve striking cannot be seen in other sports, and is something unique to kendo. For that reason, taking into account a kendoka's daily training in which he or she tries to master these movements, the difference between them and a non-kendoka was thought to be in the control of the nervous and muscular systems. With regard to manipulating the *shinai*, differences could be seen in the form of arm muscle action.

First, the basis of original kendo as combat was to "kill" the opponent using a *katana*, not a *shinai*. In a modern kendo match, that conceptual notion has not changed, but instead of killing the opponent, the goal is now connected to scoring a *yūkō-datotsu*. It could be suggested that a strike that is theoretically supposed to "kill" a person is invalid without power, whether striking *men*, *kote* or the other *datotsu-bui* (target areas). Consequently, it is thought that even if the kendoka strikes a different *datotsu-bui*, the arm power exhibited in relation to the amount of muscle action should be constant.

Second, the difference between the kendoka and non-kendoka is not only in the amount of muscle action, but also the timing for actions to start. Regarding each leg, the flexible movements of the joints are greatly affected by the action timing of the protagonistic and antagonistic muscles. For a non-kendoka who does not know how to make a correct kendo strike, their movements are clearly not smooth when observed objectively and compared with those of an experienced kendoka. This could not be made clear by video analysis, so we sought to detect electrical signals in the body through an electromyogram.

Through the use of the *shinai*, kendo has been sublimated into its present form, a sport, but nevertheless, some of its old traditions still remain. To appreciate a kendo strike is to "see tradition", and it is now considered to be connected to the ideal of personal development found in budo. The purpose of this paper is to investigate whether or not experience in kendo is a factor in the muscle action of the arms when a strike is made.

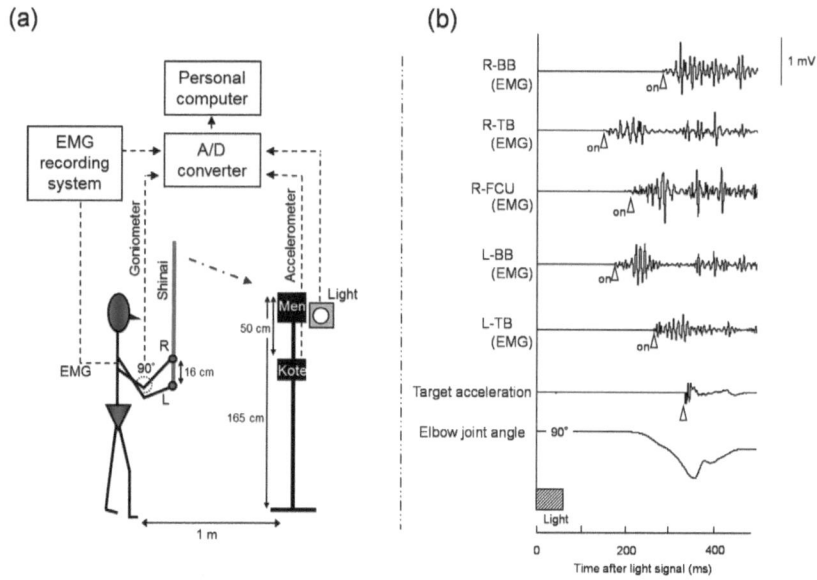

Figure 1 Schematic of experimental set-up (a) and example data (b). (a) "*Men*" represents the strike target in the *hiki-men* task, and "*Kote*" represents the strike target in the *hiki-kote* task. The subject is shown in the "ready" position adopted before the presentation of the visual cue. (b) Example data showing electromyography (EMG) recordings from the right biceps brachii (R-BB), right triceps brachii (R-TB), the left biceps brachii (L-BB), left triceps brachii (L-TB), goniometer recording from the right elbow joint, and acceleration recording from the target for a single trial.

II. Experiment Method

II-1. Test subjects and protocols

The test subjects were 14 healthy male adults (age: 23±1; height: 172.3±6.4cm; weight: 68.9±6.4kg), seven of whom were experienced kendoka (13.7±2.4 years), and seven of whom had no experience in kendo. The participants consented to take part in this study, based on the "Declaration of Helsinki", after being informed of its purpose and methods.

In this experiment, the participants were required to make *hiki-waza* strikes. An *uchikomi-dai* (a striking dummy) resembling a human body was fitted with an accelerometer (TA-513G, Nihon Kohden) on the forehead and the right wrist joint. Also, a light was fitted on the front of the *uchikomi-dai*'s head. An electro-goniometer (Model-MLTS 700, Delsys, USA) was attached to the right shoulder of the participants, and electromyogram surface electrodes were placed on their left and right biceps brachii and triceps brachii muscles. Taking into account the non-kendoka, the direction of the strikes were made along the sagittal plane and were two types of *hiki-waza*—*hiki-men* (hereafter *men*) and *hiki-kote* (hereafter *kote*). Also, in order to focus on the action of the arm muscles, all subjects were required to stand 1m away from the *uchikomi-dai*, an interval from which swinging the *shinai* (1m20cm, 510g) downwards would connect with the *men* and *kote* targets, with both elbows at a 90° angle, and strike *men* or *kote* as quickly as possible in response to a visual cue. *Men* and *kote* strikes were each made ten times. (See Fig. 1a). After the subject was confirmed to be in the ready posture, the light stimulation signal was given. Then the light stimulation signal, the electromyogram, the angle of the elbow joint and the striking power signal were recorded and fed into a personal computer (PC) through an analogue/digital (A/D) converter (16 bit, PowerLab/8sp, AD Instruments, Japan).

II-2. Electromyogram recording

The electromyogram was recorded from surface electrodes placed on the left and right biceps brachii muscles (L-BB, R-BB), the left and right triceps brachii muscles (L-TB, R-TB) and the right flexor carpal ulnaris muscle (R-FCU). Parallel bar electrodes fitted with pre-amplifiers (DE-2.1, Delsys, USA; length: 10mm; diameter: 1mm) were used, and in order to reduce skin resistance as much as possible, the subjects' arms were shaved and grease removed with rubbing alcohol on the areas where the electrodes were attached. An earth electrode was placed on the forearm's medial epicondyle of the humerus. Regarding the recording of the electromyogram, the experiment was started when a monitor checked that there was no interference and noise from neighbouring equipment. The electric signals that were derived from the electromyogram recording system (Bagnoli-8 EMG System, Delsys) were fed through an A/D converter and recorded at a sampling frequency of 2kHz, and then analysed with waveform display analysis software.

II-3. Data analysis and statistical processing

The moment of the light stimulus was identified by the light switch signal, the start of muscular electric discharge by the signals from the surface electromyography electrodes on each muscle, and the moment of strike impact by the impact reaction signals of the accelerometers fitted to the *uchikomi-dai*.

The measurement of the start of each muscle action was carried out based on the DiFabio method (1987), and the time was measured from the light stimulus to the start of the muscle action. (See Fig.1-b) Also, from the start of the muscle action to the moment of the strike,

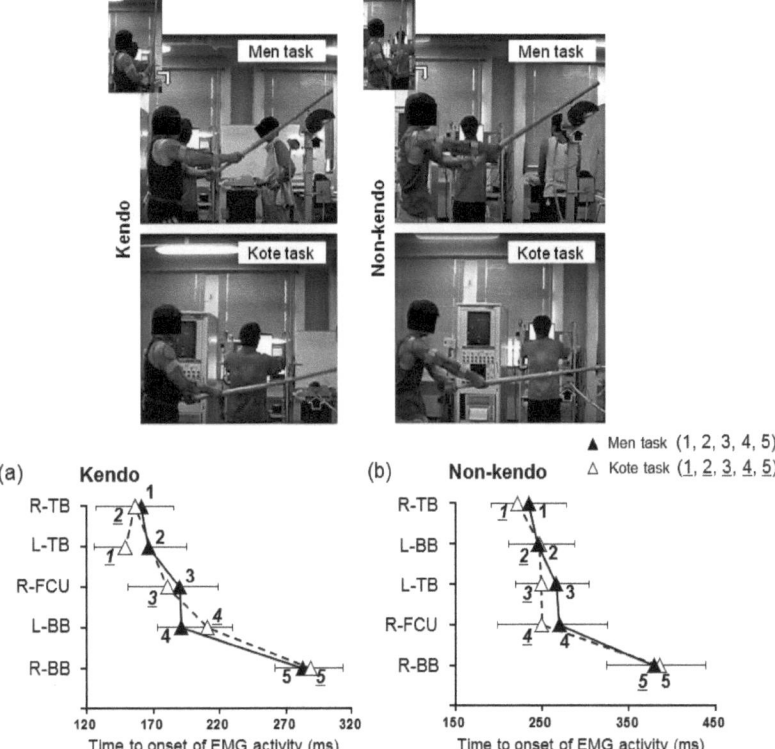

Figure 2 Sequence of EMG activity onset in the upper limbs during *hiki-men* (Men task) and *hiki-kote* (Kote task). Kendo (kendoka group); Non-kendo (non-kendoka group); BB (biceps brachii); TB (triceps brachii); FCU (flexor carpi ulnaris muscle).

the electromyogram mean amplitude (mean-RMS) was measured and the interval of the *men* and *kote* strikes compared. For the measurement data of each of the ten strikes, the average value and standard deviation of the kendoka and non-kendoka groups was calculated, and for a comparison of each movement interval, a paired t-test was conducted. The level of significance was less than 5 per cent.

III. Results and Observations

Regarding the *men* and *kote* strikes, one sample image from each of the kendoka and non-kendoka groups and the muscle action start sequence is shown in Fig.2. Looking at the images, in the non-kendoka group each strike together with the arm movement can be treated as constant, but in the kendoka group, with the trunk as the basis, in each strike the influence of the position of the left arm can be observed to be remarkably different. Accordingly, when investigating the visual stimulus that leads to the start of the sequence of muscle actions in each group, for the non-kendoka no change could be seen whether it was a *men* or *kote* strike. But for the kendoka group, because of the differences of the strikes, changes in the muscle action start sequence were indicated. That is to say, looking at the images objectively, it suggests

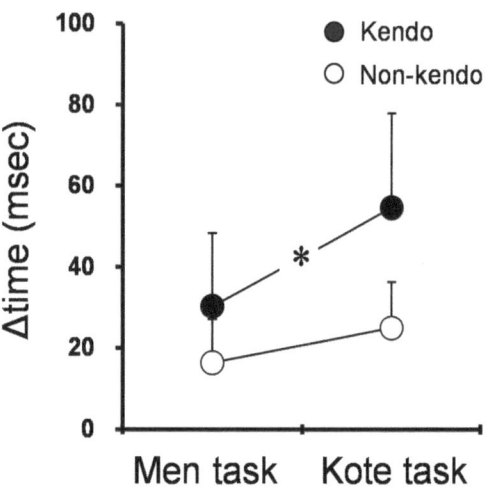
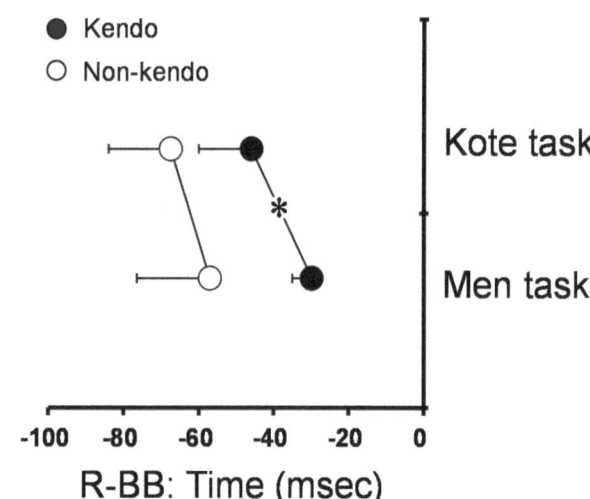

Figure 3 The time difference in EMG activity onset between the right triceps brachii and the left biceps brachii (Δ time) in the *men* and *kote* task. Abbreviations are the same as those in Figure 2. * P < 0.05.

Figure 4 Muscle activity onset time for the right biceps brachii (R-BB) in the *men* and the *kote* tasks. Abbreviations are the same as those in Figure 2. * $P < 0.05$.

that the experienced and inexperienced kendoka have differences in nerve and muscle control.

Next, the gyration of the *shinai* and its effect on the right triceps brachii and left biceps brachii muscles was investigated. Regarding the synchronous pushing of the right hand and pulling of the left, the time difference (Δ) of each muscle was calculated, and before the strike, the timing that yielded the movement of the *shinai*. The result was that in the kendoka group, *kote* was significantly longer than *men* (P < 0.05), but no difference could be seen in the non-kendoka group. (See Fig.3) In relation to the control of the *shinai*, just before the strike, the start timing of the right biceps brachii action was measured. 0 ms in Fig.4, shows the right biceps brachii start action timing for a strike. The result was that in the same way as the time difference (Δ) shown above, *kote* was notably longer than *men* for the kendoka group (P < 0.05), and for each striking interval no difference could be seen in the non-kendoka group. Therefore, regarding muscle action timing, this suggests that there are changes in the kendoka group depending on the type of strike, but not in the non-kendoka group.

Furthermore, the extent of these muscle actions was calculated, and when the *men* and *kote* strikes were compared (see Fig.5), a difference between the kendoka

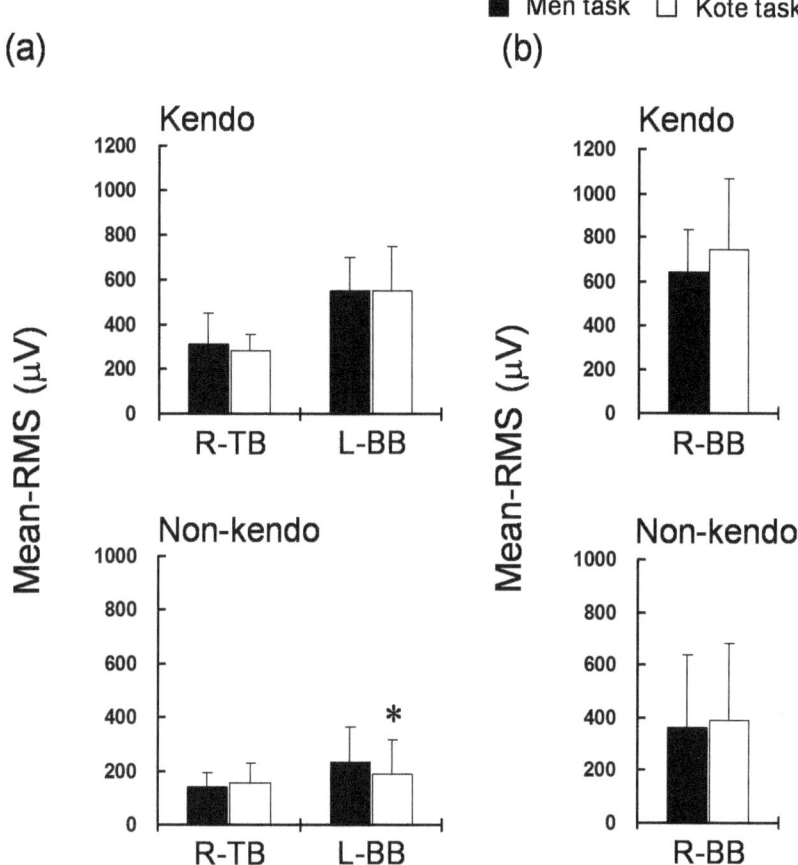

Figure 5 EMG magnitude (mean-root mean square [mean-RMS]) of the right triceps brachii (R-TB), left biceps-brachii (L-BB) and right biceps brachii (R-BB) during the men and the *kote* tasks. Abbreviations are the same as those in Figure 2. * P < 0.05 between the *men* and *kote* tasks.

group's *men* and *kote* could not be seen. For the non-kendoka group, however, a major difference was observed in relation to the movement of the *shinai* in the left biceps brachii (P < 0.05). Consequently, it is clear that the overall

tendency is for the kendoka group to change the muscle action timing depending on the strike, but on the other hand, the non-kendoka group changes the amount of muscle action. In kendo matches, the *shinai* is swung and controlled precisely in a short time, so it is an important skill to make the repeated striking movements smoother (Kobayashi, 1966). In this study, taking into account the muscle action timing and with regard to the lower striking location of *kote* than *men*, in the kendoka group the *shinai* is not swung and controlled with the same timing as *men*. The timing of the strike is counterbalanced by its position. Additionally, strikes with a foundation of trying "to kill" are executed by non-kendoka by regulating their power (amount of muscle action) with each strike, but with the experienced kendoka a change cannot be seen. Through the results of this paper and prior research (Tsuboi, 1968; 1973), we have come to understand that in strikes peculiar to kendo, the muscle action of the arms is influenced by the presence or absence of experience in kendo.

IV. Conclusion

This research compared and investigated the patterns of arm muscle actions in *hiki-men* and *hiki-kote* strikes for experienced and inexperienced kendoka. The results show that the muscle action start sequence is different for both groups, with the kendoka group changing depending on whether the strike is *men* or *kote*. Furthermore, regarding the muscle action pattern when moving and controlling the *shinai*, the kendoka group's muscle action timing changed, but in the non-kendoka group the amount of muscle action changed. These contrasting results can be explained by the presence or absence of kendo experience.

References

- DiFabio R.P., (1987) "Reliability of computerized surface electromyography for determining the onset of muscle activity", *Phys. Ther.*, 67, 43-48.
- Kobayashi K., (1966) "*Kendō ni okeru dageki nitsuite*" (A consideration of striking in kendo), *Journal of Health, Physical Education and Recreation*, 16, 656-660. [in Japanese]
- Ono M., Otani Y., Takahashi Y., Tsubota S. and Kurata H. (1968) "Study on the neuro-muscular coordinations of the kendo champions (Part 1)", *Japanese Journal of Physical Fitness and Sports Medicine*, 17, 1-13. [in Japanese]
- Ono M., Yanagimoto A., Yamashita F. and Kurata H. (1969) "Study on the neuro-muscular coordination of the kendo champions (Part 2)", *Japanese Journal of Physical Fitness and Sports Medicine*, 18, 72-82. [in Japanese]
- Tsuboi S., (1968) "Study of the Position of the Electromyogram on Hitting Motion in Japanese Fencing", *Japanese Journal of Physical Fitness and Sports Medicine*, 17, 155. [in Japanese]
- Tsuboi S., (1973) "A Study on the Dynamic Postures in 'Kendo': An Experimental Analysis of the Basic Blowing Actions", *Japan Society of Physical Education*, 18. 71-81. [in Japanese]

MARIO BOTTONI'S LEGACY

By Donatella Castelli

Not many are familiar with the history of Italian kendo. Some older European kenshi remember a rather tormented history of multiple federations, but nowadays, no one wonders why the Italian Kendo Renmei is called CIK (Italian Kendo Confederation), even though its current organisational structure does not resemble a confederation. In this article I wish to remember one of the protagonists in the history of Italian kendo: Mario Bottoni.

Mario Bottoni was one of the first pioneers who started kendo practice in Italy. He was not alone in those humble beginnings, but he stood out for his strength of personality, and even more for his ideas. Strong personalities abound in the kendo world, but Mario Bottoni was a tough cookie. His pursuit for the profound nature of kendo was tireless. In the early 1970s, aspiring Italian kenshi had to put up with a scarcity of proper teaching (some Japanese sensei appear much later in our story) and with a lack of equipment. Those were the days, lasting well into the 1980s, in which splintered *shinai* were "repaired" with sticky tape. Practice was hard, and brute strength was often considered a valid substitute for technique.

Mario believed that kendo had to be preserved as close as possible to its nature—a nature ingrained in Japanese culture and spirit, and without concessions to the sporting trends that brought judo adrift, even in Japan. In those early days, Mario fought to defend those principles and integrity against anyone, gathering companions along the way and creating the first organised group in Italian kendo, the AIK (Italian Kendo Association).

The AIK immediately found itself in the line of fire with the Italian National Olympic Committee, as they wished to include this "new thing from Japan" in their catalogue. Some so-called sports manager saw himself crowned as the lifelong president of this new entity, with honours, authority, and a budget to go with it.

It was a very hard fight—purity against personal gain. It was an uneven fight, too, that seemed lost at a certain point. Luckily, an alliance was formed with a newborn federation (FeNIKe), which created enough power to keep the sport sharks at bay. It was not plain sailing for a long time; having been the third president of the Italian Kendo Confederation, I was a very much involved witness to the harshness of the political confrontation. The prize we were all fighting for was recognition from the International Kendo Federation, which was eventually bestowed on CIK (the confederation born out of the AIK and FeNIKe) in 1988.

During these painful years of unrest, the CIK started to create a complex network of relationships that allowed the technical and spiritual growth of Italian kenshi, and the fruits are visible today. The CIK has grown from being the unhappy marriage of two not-so-willing partner entities into a fully-fledged, homogeneous federation. The CIK is still independent and self-funded, and it has grown to be the third-biggest European federation. It also hosted the 15th World Kendo Championships, and regularly offers a great range of opportunities to its members: seminars and tournaments fill the calendar, Japanese and also Korean sensei come freely and regularly to visit, and the clubs prosper and grow.

None of this would have been possible if Mario Bottoni had not kept his relentless stance regarding the nature of kendo, and about the proper attitude to teach, learn and train. He was certainly controversial, and the AIK was considered elitist: its members had to practise hard, develop a knowledge of kendo's principles and integrate in the spirit of the group from the very beginning. Consciousness was the keyword—not practise to perspire, but aspire to self-improvement. Mario prepared many manuals, handbooks and synopses. There was an AIK newsletter, painstakingly assembled in the days in which personal computing was not the norm. Practice in the dojo had to go hand-in-hand with culture, but it was not for everyone.

It seems strange to recall now, but kendo was a battlefield not only in the dojo, but also on paper or in meetings, both in Italy and Europe. Having been Mario's successor as president of the AIK, I had to take on some of those fights myself, all the way to the EKF General Assembly, as some still remember.

Mario left us a year ago. He was 84. He reached the rank of 4-dan and never accepted titles such as "Maestro", that some others were too eager to wear, having done much less than what Mario did for Italian kendo. It has to be said that even some of those who were closest to him got tired of fighting and turned their backs on him, as soon as they saw a safe shore to land on. Nevertheless, the legacy of Mario is more up-to-date than ever.

At the WKC in Paris in 1994, Mario distributed a pamphlet about what the WKC had grown into: a juggernaut event, requiring large halls, luxury hotels, and professional organisation. He denounced this, prophesising the increased difficulty for less well-off countries to organise, or even to take part in this type of event. His criticisms went all the way to the International Kendo Federation (IKF), which he thought had embraced a fully Westernised Olympic-like approach for kendo. Mario was accused of raining on international kendo's parade, and there was an angry reaction to his observations. But today more than ever, after almost 20 years, we are still discussing the issue. If the German Kendo Federation had to charge its team to take part in the 2013 European Kendo Championships simply because the budget would not be sufficient otherwise, was Mario too far from the mark? Some have even criticised the IKF for having to change its name to FIK to be accepted into SportAccord, and its participation in the World Combat Games just to have the right to represent kendo throughout the world (which is a fact that could have been overshadowed by a rogue World Kendo Federation, one with a bigger flair for appearances). This is not so far from the future prophesised by Mario in his pamphlet.

It is a common feeling, in Europe at least, that kendo is better off far from the Olympic Games—a beautiful ideal appealing to everyone, that has been inseparably intertwined with business: sponsorships, exclusive TV rights, and product placement. Maybe it does not take a big effort to see how far this is from "kendo", and Mario saw this coming in the 1970s. He urged all kenshi not to be dazzled by the grandeur of the organisation, or by the myth of the gold medallist. Kendo is about selflessness, modesty and respect—nothing to do with champion worship or adoring crowds. His lesson is still current and it should be learnt by the new generations of kenshi.

Shinai Saga
The Coil

By Charlie Kondek

When Takeo Murata bowed, it was with the grace of generations at his shoulders, and it looked very natural, a small, easy movement he had made thousands of times since childhood. The same movement, by Jeff Graham, still seemed stiff and unaligned after 20 years. But both men raised their *shinai* to the *taitō* position at the hip with the same efficiency, and the observable differences between them dissolved when they squatted in *sonkyo* with the *kensen* of their weapons inches apart.

Graham was the first to *kiai*. As a beginner, when kendo had been alien to him, he'd learned to *kiai* to embolden himself, to make what was then a frightening, disorienting state manageable. He had begun his combats with a sudden *kiai* so consistently that it had become habit, the door by which he always entered. Murata answered but his *kiai* was different. In the first place, it was not so immediate. But it was also calmer than Graham's, less urgent. Contained. Murata performed a different habit at the outset of the contest, and could almost hear, in his mind, the admonishment of the old sensei from his school days, barking at him and the other pupils for taking a small step to the right as they rose from *sonkyo*. "Why do you do that? All of you? Stop it! Stay in the centre. Don't move to the right." Even now, almost thirty years later, Murata, rising, had to fight to keep from stepping to his right.

Their *kensen* crossed. Murata was filled with a sense of esteem for his opponent, an estimation that included himself. Graham thought more of his own plans and preferences, though he was of course aware of Murata. In Graham's calculations, he, Graham, was the integer, his *waza* the numbers known. Murata was the variable, and Graham was thinking, "What do I have to multiply, what divide, to get the product I want?" Murata, on his side, felt the gaps in his skill level caused by his many absences from training. Part of him watched Graham carefully to suggest a counter-strategy, but part of him also wondered how much of his old skill and energy would be available to him tonight.

Murata would never have put it this way, but as a fencer he often felt haunted by the ghost of the one he had been as a younger man, as if that distinct entity lived in his body sometimes, made itself known, inhabited him or corners of him and then retreated to the attic in his mind. This was a stronger, faster, more graceful Murata, a Murata whom the *shinai* and the body obeyed. But it was different than the Murata that now pressed his *kensen* toward Graham's throat, brushing at his *shinai*. Not that he had ever been a great champion, just that in his college years he had been at a pinnacle of ability. It seemed to him now that he'd had more energy then, and when he willed himself to a certain place, willed the whip snap cut of his *kensen* to the crown of his opponent's *men*, the body and the weapon did not follow as they once had, or as he imagined they once had, but moved, as if through a gauze, resisting the path of his sword in its plunge, softening its impact against his opponent's lifted, deflecting *shinai*.

Graham loved *taiatari*. That was a characteristic of his style, common to many of the men in his dojo that, like him, had begun kendo as an adult and never quite developed the springiness, the swerve, that years of youthful *kakari-geiko* might have developed. No, Graham executed good, straight *waza*, but he liked to slam into his opponent afterward and lean into him, perhaps let the impact carry him backward a few steps. To him, a large percentage of the attack culminated in that impact after a cut. He did not move past or through his opponent as someone like Murata did.

Frankly, Graham felt there was something ugly about his kendo and always would be. He compared his own body and way of standing and walking to the Japanese. The length of his muscled arms, disproportionate to his short legs, was nearly simian, as were his broad shoulders and wide torso with its gently plummeting, middle aged abdomen. He also bore a head and beard of red-gold hair, but it seemed to Graham that no amount of earnest training in *chūdan-no-kamae* could transform him into a shape as elegant, as fitted to kendo, as the Japanese. When he cut, he cut well, fundamentally, but the impact and follow-through of his attacks, the *zanshin*, lacked the arrowing grace of his counterparts among them. Even the way his back and buttocks filled out the *hakama* was different. His legs bent as he cut and his body thundered, unlike Murata's, blade thin, composed, drawing a line that sloped upward from the left toe to the tip of the sword, whereas Graham's drew a capital S: toes, legs, chest, shoulders, and outstretched arms.

It was under the lip of this wave that Murata's *dō*, precisely placed and loud as a pistol, now sliced. Was it the ghost of Murata, Murata himself, or the man haunted and inhabited by the ghost that guided the timing, the angled steps of the feet, the twist of hips and shoulders? In Graham's 20 years of kendo the offering of *men* and the receiving of *dō* was a not uncommon transaction; the same could not be said for the reverse. Men like Graham worked hard to develop the *men* cut, then moved on to *kote* and *kote-men* – the *dō* remained elusive, particularly in a setting in which the harmonious *ai-uchi* attack or the sniping *debana* was more natural. Graham could only complete the exchange, admire the *dō* as it passed him, acknowledge it when he turned with a small nod of his head and a spoken "*arigatou*", which was returned. It was the very picture of kendo.

Both men renewed their concentration. Each had left a great deal of concern outside the dojo. The hands that gripped Graham's sword were the hands of a carpenter, a tradesman, and had worked for most of his post-college career in the shop of a small but respected fabricator specialising in customized signage, shelters and uniquely shaped products for retail or marketing events. He had found his way into the work making sets, props and costumes at his university's theatre department, and had over the years gone from being a "mule" and general craftsman to a specifier, producer, project manager. He had always kept company with the offbeat and the artistic; it was an attitude that had lead him to kendo, actually. But his company had increasingly taken on more sophisticated digital assignments for which it was ill-suited, text-to-screen displays, responsive video games and things like that. Graham had begun to wonder if he hadn't outgrown, or had the potential to outgrow his employer. He had already been approached by competing firms and toyed with the idea of going into business for himself.

The company he worked for fit like a well-worn work shirt, old and patched. It had been a staple of the local advertising community for decades and was on its second generation of ownership. Parking in the dirt lot every day and entering the warehouse to the smell of coffee, sawdust and lacerated plastic still evoked in Graham the magical feelings that had set him on this rewarding path nearly 20 years ago. He was in his 40s now. He had two children. Part of him wondered if moving on to a new professional phase didn't constitute some much needed growing up. He couldn't make custom beer tents and fibreglass body parts forever. And yet, even entertaining the idea of leaving felt like a kind of betrayal. Hadn't he ought to instead take on more of a leadership role, to try and nudge the company toward a new paradigm? Or, wouldn't another employer teach him what he needed, give him contacts he didn't have? The hands that gripped the *tsuka* of Graham's sword were the large, calloused hands of a workman, but behind the eyes that flicked from his opponent's *shinai* to his face lurked a mind that grappled with decisions, some distant, some near.

The hands that held Murata's sword, indistinguishable from Graham's within identical *kote*, were the hands of a banker. He worked in the financial department of a large international manufacturer, and his button-down days were filled with consensus-seeking meetings and poring over endless documentation of regulations. His ability with language as much as with figures had brought him to the U.S., and he liked it here; as busy and monotonous as the work could be, it was not as overwhelming as business life in Japan, not nearly. They did things differently here. Better, maybe.

Murata's return to kendo, practised all through his school days and set aside as his career had taken hold, still surprised him. He still pondered the impulse that had made him take it up again after 17 years, fascinated that the opportunity would present itself after so much time and so far from his origins. Maybe that more than anything was what lead him back. Maybe he had intended to return all along. What emotion or logic was it that drew him, he wondered; certainly he believed kendo was "good for him," physically and psychologically. But perhaps there was a lingering, beckoning feeling of obligation, a need. Perhaps kendo reunited him with something essential that had been missing in his life, something to which God or karma had always intended him to return. What was it?

Some part of Murata's subconscious mind worked at it while his conscious mind dealt with Graham's attack against his *men*. It seemed to him as he struck up and against Graham's *shinai* that kendo was a thing he at first pursued but which now pursued him. Perhaps he would unravel its method and meaning one day. Perhaps he would become content with its mystery. Graham, because of his artistic training, was familiar with the interplay of conscious and subconscious. As he pressed Murata, initiated another attack to Murata's *men*, then revealed the feint that exposed Murata's *kote*, he was faintly aware that he had thrown his professional dilemma into the black engine of un-thinking while devoting his attention to dropping his wrists, hips, and the tip of his *shinai* to the target. Graham claimed his prize with a triumphant shout and a movement of *zanshin* that thrust his belly,

chest and shoulders into Murata's, their chins inches apart with the bars of both masks between them. This time, it was Murata's turn to nod.

The opponents backed apart, squared themselves. Graham pulled air into his chest, thrust it down into his belly, pushed his shoulders back and tensed his left leg. Murata relaxed his hands, then let them drop and press over the back of the *tsuka*, let the *kensen* fall just a little, and with it the stomach, the hips, the right knee. Though each man in his composure isolated different parts of the body, different aspects of the identical stance, the same intention pounded in each heart and throbbed in each vein: cut him in such a way that he can't cut me. The mechanism that ignited the spark, that turned the gears, that pumped breath and blood and drove them forward was one that had been crafted, was being crafted still, by teachers and peers, by persistent programming, discipline and effort. Perhaps none of these forces exerted as great an influence as each individual himself. Certainly, both Graham and Murata had been instructed that kendo is best developed by one's own realisation of things.

Now each probed, made his different plans. If I move here, will he open there? If I cut this way, will he have time to cover, or counter, or dodge; will it leave me open to a cut of his? How deep should I step? Should I vary my timing? Retreat to draw him in? Graham roared his enormous, red-bearded *kiai*. Murata replied; curt, restrained.

Confusion Regarding *Waza* among Beginner Kendoka

By Thomas Sluyter

This article describes my research process in creating the recent "Waza Explained" article, and its accompanying media, on the Renshinjuku Kendo Dojo website.[1]

All beginnings are hard
The first few years of training in kendo provide the student with a veritable onslaught of new things to learn. Between new body movements, etiquette, weird clothing and the Japanese language, kendo certainly provides a steep learning curve for the average Westerner. I spent my first year getting to grips with my body, thoroughly acquainted to office work as it was, trying to achieve some semblance of the movements displayed by my *sempai*.

In my second year, having graduated to club *bōgu*, I worked hard in class and participated in a few tournaments. I was at that particular stage where one has no understanding of *seme*, *tame* or any of the *waza*. Wild swings and no "dialogue" with my opponent are what I displayed at the time. Of course, sensei showed us many techniques during class, which I dutifully copied, but I had no inkling of how to practically apply anything beyond simple big or small strikes.

A first introduction to kendo *waza*
Even in my first year I spent many hours reading magazines, essays and glossaries, among them Masahiro Imafuji-sensei's "Kendo Technique Guide".[2] I always appreciated that particular webpage, as it had a list of the most common *waza* and a simple diagram showing the divide between *shikake* and *ōji-waza*. Imafuji-sensei's list provided me with the names and a short, clear description of each technique.

Despite having read so much theory, I could not unify it with the practical part of kendo. Until then I had always practised these *waza* in a vacuum: watch a short demonstration, practise it ten times, then move on to the next *waza*. And to me, like many beginners, the demonstrations often looked very much alike. "*Sensei caught that blow and retaliated with his own strike! But was that kaeshi or suriage?!*"

With my *shodan* exam on the way I felt it was time to start applying these techniques. In order to do so, I had to tackle the three biggest weak spots in my current understanding:

- Analyse the physical aspects. What exactly does the *waza* look like?
- Research the underlying reasoning. Why does one use this particular *waza*?
- What are the differences between the various *waza*? What sets them apart?

Because I am a firm proponent of the sharing of information I decided to compile my findings in an article for my dojo's website. Thus I hoped not only to benefit myself, but also my classmates.

Find the differences: Spotting the *waza*
I am a visual learner, meaning that sketching things helps me to memorise new information. That is why I loved Imafuji-sensei's explanations so much: the simple "mind map" diagram. Hence my research process centred around the creation of a comparative table, outlining various characteristics of *waza*. Starting with the *waza* descriptions provided by Imafuji-sensei and Salmon-sensei,[3] I started checking boxes.

The division between *shikake* and *ōji-waza* had already been made, but while reading through various resources, I soon discovered two other distinguishing aspects to *waza* which could very easily be added to the table:

1. *San-sappō* ("three killing methods")
2. *Sen* ("opening move" or "initiative")

In my understanding, *sen* is a matter of timing and of initiative, and it describes how your actions relate to those of your opponent. *San-sappō* describes how each particular *waza* achieves success, by "killing" either your opponent's spirit, sword, or technique. I will not go further into these concepts as they have been explained by many great teachers, including articles in volumes 5.2[4] and 6.2[5] of *Kendo World*. Unfortunately, most of those materials went over my head when I first read them in 2011-2012, but piecing things together for my table made things a lot clearer!

Further extending my studies into other budo, such as karate[6] and aikido[7], strengthened my comprehension of *sen*.

Table 1

waza	Type		Sansappo			... no sen		
	shikake	oji	ki	ken	waza	sen sen	sen	go
renzoku	×					×		
hiki	×					×		
katsugi	×		×			×		
hikibana	×		×			×		
seme	×		×			×		
harai	×			×		×		
osae	×			×		×		
maki	×			×		×		
debana	×				×		×	
uchiotoshi		×		×	×			×
kiriotoshi		×			×			×
nuki		×			×			×
suriage		×			×			×
kaeshi		×			×			×

Figure 1

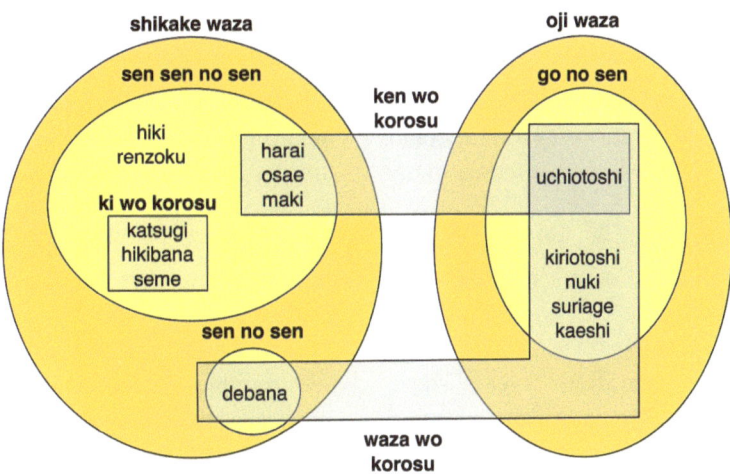

For example it taught me why aikido still considers *sensen-no-sen* to be a defensive, as opposed to an aggressive, action. To paraphrase Goodin-sensei on *sensen-no-sen*: groining your opponent so he cannot begin to attack you is still a defensive move.[6]

Given my beginner-level understanding of kendo, I had made a few mistakes in my first draft of the table, which were quickly ironed out with Salmon-sensei's help. The end result is as follows. (*see* Table 1.)

Having compiled the comparative table, it was then a relatively small step to gather the *waza* into a Venn diagram. Based on the table, I grouped the *waza* on a sheet of paper and then I started pencilling the lines. The end result is shown here. (*see* Figure 1.)

From there on, my research focused on analysing the differences between individual *waza* which, though seemingly similar, are not at all alike. The full article may be read online.[7] The body of the article consists of the following comparisons:

- *Nuki* versus *debana*
- *Kaeshi* versus *suriage*
- *Suriage* versus *harai*
- *Seme* versus *osae* versus *harai*

For example:

"*Nuki* versus *debana* - What's the difference between a *nuki-kote* and a *debana-kote*? During *keiko* they may feel the same to most beginners. They see sensei square up against a victim, the victim does an attack and sensei whacks him before the attack lands. The table above should make the biggest difference clear: timing. *Men-nuki-kote*, or more commonly *men-nuki-dō*, is performed by evading a strike that is already on its way to you. *Debana-kote* and so on, are done before your opponent has even started attacking. Right before he attacks, you do. It is a matter of *sen*, from "*sen wo toru*", "to anticipate".

Where *debana-waza* are "*sen-no-sen*", *nuki-waza* are "*go-no-sen*". With the former you sense that your opponent is going to act and you counteract at the same time. With the latter you can still prevent your opponent's action from succeeding by blocking and then attacking. *Ai-men* is also "*sen-no-sen*". [...] The remaining *ōji-waza* are all "*go-no-sen*": *suriage, kaeshi* and *uchiotoshi*."

The difference between these two techniques is illustrated in the table and Venn diagram.

Feedback from my peers
Based on the initial reactions, I was doing something right, as they were usually along the lines of "I finally get it!" or "Clearest explanation I've read so far!" What this suggests to me is that a lot of beginners who are starting to learn *waza* could benefit from more theoretical groundwork. I recall reading an explanation of differing (kendo) learning styles between Japan and the West. In Japan one supposedly learns by doing, while in the West, one wants to first understand what we are going to be doing and why. The reactions to my article seem to support this.

It is not my place to suggest changes to kendo training regimen, so instead I would like to submit these ideas for your consideration:

- Encourage students and kohai, from an early stage, to study and discuss kendo theory. It has been often suggested that learning kendo is more than just a physical journey.
- When demonstrating *waza*, consider demonstrating what sets them apart from other techniques.
- Do not shun technical discussions with lower ranked students. They may not fully grasp the subject matter, but it will be a learning experience nonetheless.

Feedback from my superiors
A short while after publishing the article, I also received feedback from higher-graded sempai and sensei from across the globe. Their reception of my summary was not as enthusiastic as that of my peers.

- Person A was surprised that beginners could ever confuse *nuki-waza* and *debana-waza*, stating that the difference should be obviously clear. He also prefers to learn techniques on the floor, as opposed to reading about them. While he also finds the research laudable, he suggests that such learning is not required at the lower ranks.
- Person B provided a wealth of technical discussion adding to the comparisons I had originally made. One of the bigger points he stressed is that he disagreed between the sharp distinction that I appear to make between *shikake-waza* and *ōji-waza*. He also warned that my inclusion of *seme-waza* could confuse some beginners who may think that I am referring to "*seme*" itself. He also finds that breaking things down based on *san-sappō* is fruitless, insofar that one should always strive to attack all three of your opponent's strong points.
- Person C posited that my approach is fundamentally flawed and that the article would have been a lot more useful had I based it on primary materials (after studying Japanese), instead of relying on second- or third-hand materials as I did. My article is missing background regarding both the history and philosophy of *waza* and the classifications thereof.

I am very grateful to all these teachers as their feedback has provided me with a lot of things to work on. Not only will I improve upon the original article by updating the discussions therein, but I have also been shown new things to investigate.

Where to from here?
Preparing for this article has provided me with a number of new questions to answer and new avenues to explore. For example, Nakano-sensei writes that *go-no-sen* not only applies to the finishing of a physical technique, but also to faltering *seme*.[4] Therefore, *shikake-waza* could also be applied as *go-no-sen*, as opposed to what my current table suggests. Similarly, Stroud-sensei[5] suggests that simple *renzoku-waza* could be used to "kill the *waza*" in *sensen-no-sen*, which is something that befuddles me. And of course there is the wealth of feedback provided by my superiors to take into account.

As always, kendo will continue to provide us all with interesting challenges and mysteries to investigate!

1 Sluyter, T. "Waza explained", Renshinjuku Kendo Dojo website (2013)—http://www.renshinjuku.nl/2013/10/waza-explained/
2 Imafuji, M. "Kendo technique guide", Kendo-Guide.com (2008-2011)—http://www.kendo-guide.com/kendo_techniques.html
3 Salmon, G. "Kendo: a comprehensive guide to Japanese swordsmanship" (ISBN 978-1-4629-1180-6, 2013)
4 Nakano, Y. "Striking opportunities & San-Sappo", *Kendo World Journal* (Vol. 5 No. 2, 2010), pp. 66-68.
5 Stroud, R.D. "The concept of San Satsu Hō and its relationship to Mittsu no Sen", *Kendo World Journal* (Vol. 6 No. 2), pp. 10-12
6 Goodin, C.C. "Making sense of sen", Karate Thoughts Blog (2006) - http://karatejutsu.blogspot.nl/2006/05/making-sense-of-sen.html
7 Weisgard, E.M. "The art of timing", Aiki Shuren Dojo website (2005) - http://www.aiki-shuren-dojo.com/pdf/Go%20no%20sen.pdf

NITO

By Yamaguchi Masato

Kendo is usually done with one *shinai*, so *nitō* has been treated with relative indifference. Also, because *nitō* was excluded from official competitions in the post-war period, the number of instructors and students able to carry it on has decreased. As the appearance of the *nitō* style is completely different from one *shinai* (*ittō* style), some kendo experts tend to view *nitō* with scepticism. *nitō* does however also lend many useful things to the practice of *ittō*, and it can also be used as another route to reach the ultimate goal of kendo.

A Japanese proverb states "Even if you chase two rabbits at the same time, you cannot catch both of them." It means that you cannot have everything if you are greedy. *Nitō* is often made fun of with this proverb because the Japanese pronunciation of the word '*nitō*' meaning 'two rabbits' and 'two swords' is similar. However, an acquisitive approach may actually result in a kind of synergy. One may be able to get more benefit than trying to catch one rabbit by thinking about the methods to catch many rabbits. But, if you go about *nitō* the wrong way, it could be the first step to ruining your kendo.

I would ask that readers understand there is more than one style of *nitō* and so there may be differences. I think it is important that you consider the techniques of *nitō* in a rational and logical fashion, maintaining a degree of open-mindedness. I think freedom of creativity is one of the fascinations of *nitō*.

There is little information about *nitō* in English. (Even in Japanese there is not much available). What I have written here should act as an introduction for those looking at *nitō* for the first time. This is by no means supposed to be a definitive work and should not be used in lieu of a qualified sensei. My focus is to show the technical aspects of *nitō*, not an in-depth background history that I feel has nothing to do with practising *nitō*.

There are many different ways of practising some elements of nitō, such as how to hold the sword, etiquette and so forth. The author is teaching from his experience, which demonstrates one of the possible legitimate methods for nitō.

PART 7: Practical Techniques

1. Against the Various Types of *Kamae*

• **Against *Hira-seigan***

Hira-seigan may be one of the most effective *kamae* against *nitō*. (Figure 1-1) For the *nitō* practitioner, it is difficult to neutralize the *shinai* with the *shōtō*, and also the position of the *shinai* (left hand is on the centreline) is offensive. This *kamae* guards the right *kote* with the *shinai*, so it is difficult to strike *kote* without using diagonal footwork to do so.

When facing *hira-seigan*, position the *shōtō* where it is easy to cross the opponent's *shinai* (*kiri-musubi*). The *kiri-musubi* will be the key to the attack. *Seme* to the left with the *shōtō*, slide the *shōtō* along the opponent's *shinai* and strike with the *daitō* when the motion stops. *Nitō* beginners are quick to try to push the opponent's *shinai* with the *shōtō*, but the primary thing you have to neutralise is not the *shinai*, but the spirit.

Figure 1-1 *hira-seigan*.

Orthodox *Sei-Nitō*

Men Strike

From *sei-nitō*, the *men* appears open to attack, so it seems easy to strike. However, the *ittō* player is ready for this, so you need to be careful when you choose to strike. Try to get close to the opponent, and strike *men* while holding the opponent's *shinai* down to the left. You should make this *men* strike by taking one step from your left foot. If you find that you cannot get close enough to the opponent or you cannot find an opportunity to strike, you may try a *men* strike with two steps forward from the right foot. (Figure 1-2)

Kote Strike

From *sei-nitō*, the *kote* is hidden by the *shinai*. Therefore, the *kote* strike is used as an opening for the next strike or when the opponent focuses on a *men* strike. Once their arms are raised, strike *kote* quickly from the right foot. (Figure 1-3)

Figure 1-2 *sei-nitō* men strike against *hira-seigan*.

Figure 1-3 *sei-nitō* kote strike against *hira-seigan*.

Gyaku-nitō

Men Strike

From *gyaku-nitō*, it appears difficult to strike both *men* and *kote* because they are on the same side as the *daitō*. Because of this, the concept of *kiri-musubi* will become more important. Remember the point of *kiri-musubi* is the place that spirit, sword, and body are crossed. Try to cross your *shōtō* and the opponent's *shinai*. When you feel you have reached the point of *kiri-musubi*, strike *men* quickly from the right foot. (Figure 1-4)

Kote Strike

Once you have reached the point of *kiri-musubi*, the opponent feels the pressure or fear that a *men* strike is coming. They will tend to raise their arms easily in this situation, so take advantage of this and strike their *kote* from the left at that moment, with the left foot. (Figure 1-5)

Figure 1-4 *Gyaku-nitō men* strike against *hira-seigan*.

Figure 1-5 *Gyaku-nitō kote* strike against *hira-seigan*.

- **Against *Kasumi***

You do not need to worry too much about *kasumi* (*ittō*) because this *kamae* is defensive and the left hand is off the centerline. (Figure 1-6) Compared with *chūdan*, the *ittō* player does not need to worry about the *shōtō*, but their left *kote* becomes a valid target. As with *hira-seigan*, the basic strategy with your *kamae* for *kasumi* is to situate the *shōtō* where you can easily cross the point of gravity of your *shōtō* and the opponent's *shinai* (*kiri-musubi*). You should have an intention and feeling of upwards *seme* with the *shōtō*. Calm your spirit down and deal with the opponent.

Kasumi is used to defend the right side. It is often used against *jōdan* and *gyaku-nitō*. For a normal *nitō* player, every target is open and easy to attack, but watch for some traps.

Gyaku-Nitō
Men Strike
Carefully try to get close to the opponent, and strike *men* while holding the opponent's *shinai* upwards. This *men* strike is made with one step from the right foot. If you find that you cannot get close enough to the opponent or you cannot find an opportunity to strike, you may try a *men* strike with two steps forward from the left foot. (Figure 1-7)

Kote Strike
The right *kote* of the opponent will be difficult to strike because *ittō kasumi* is designed to protect the right side. Similar to *men*, strike the left *kote* by crossing your arms. (Figure 1-8)

Figure 1-6 *Kasumi-no-kamae*

Figure 1-7 *Gyaku-nitō men* strike against *kasumi*.

Figure 1-8 *Gyaku-nitō kote* strike against *kasumi*.

Actual *gyaku-nitō kote* strike from the left foot.

Dō Strike

Because of the nature of this *kamae*, it is easy to get the *kasumi* opponent to raise their arms. In this case, strike *dō*. Remember, however, not to strike *dō* without first doing *seme* to the *kote* and/or *men*. (Figure 1-9)

Figure 1-9 *Gyaku-nitō dō* strike against *kasumi*.

• **Against *jōdan***

Nitō is very good at handling attacks from above. Even if your opponent does not know much about *jōdan*, they still sometimes try to use it against *nitō*. The first impulse when up against *nitō* seems to be to take *jōdan*. A *nitō* practitioner uses *jūji-no-kamae* against *jōdan*. The *daitō* is held underneath the *shōtō*, paying attention to the angle and direction of the blade (*ha*) of the *shōtō*. With an attacking spirit, strike *kote* (*men*) and *tsuki* by pushing the *daitō* down with the *shōtō*. When the opponent strikes first, receive the attack with *jūji-no-kamae* (*jūji-uke*) and respond with a strike. When you attack first, always push the *daitō* with the *shōtō*. A big step forward is also important. The same as above, strike short-distance techniques from the foot on the *shōtō* side, and for longer distance attacks, from the foot on the *daitō* side. It goes without saying that when a *jōdan* player lowers their *shinai*, you may strike *men*. (Figure 1-11~1-14)

Figure 1-10 *jōdan-no-kamae*

Figure 1-11 *Gyaku-nitō* right *kote* strike against *jōdan*.

Figure 1-12 *Gyaku-nitō* left *kote* strike against *jōdan*.

Figure 1-14 *Gyaku-nitō tsuki* thrust against *jōdan*.

- **Against *Nitō***

The strategy against a *nitō* player is similar to that for *ai-jōdan* (both sides are taking *jōdan-no-kamae*). Position the *shōtō* where it is difficult for the opponent to strike your *men*. In general, *nitō* players are good at defence, so attack well and try to find and take advantage of the chances you get.

Men Strike

Try to attack from both the left and right, and move both *shinai* around to confuse the opponent. Strike when the opponent focuses on your *shōtō* - do not miss this opportunity. When you succeed in getting in close to the opponent, try to strike from the foot on the *shōtō* side. If necessary, you can also strike from the other foot. The figure shows the latter case. (Figure 1-15)

Kote Strike

This strike is difficult to achieve, but visualise and practise hard to master it as it is very effective when done well. (Figure 1-16)

Dō Strike

When you keep attacking the *men* and *kote*, *dō* may sometimes open up as both *men* and *kote* are attacked from above. Seize the chance when it comes. The *dō* strike surprises the opponent but you will be defenseless after the strike, so do not use it too often. (Figure 1-17)

Figure 1-13 *Gyaku-nitō dō* strike against *jōdan*.

Figure 1-15 *Sei-nitō men* strike against *gyaku-nitō*.

Figure 1-17 *Sei-nitō dō* strike against *gyaku-nitō*.

2. Types of Opponents

I would like to introduce some impressive types of players that I have practised with. As mentioned above, most players try to use *jōdan* or *hira-seigan* to beat *nitō*.

• Speedy type

If the *ittō* opponent has the same level of skill as the *nitō* practitioner, the *ittō* side has an advantage in both power and speed. When the opponent is fast and it is difficult to find a break in their timing, make an opening to let them strike. Then you can respond to this easily when they take the bait. Even if your strike is not perfect, try to confuse them. This will lead them to restrict their own movements.

• Power Type

Those who are confident of their power try to crush *nitō* with it. They use more power than necessary, but remember that the underlying concept of *nitō* is *sotai-wa*. The more powerful the opponent is, the more harmonious and responsive you must be.

• Fleeing Type (*sansho-yoke*)

The way of escaping with a raised left hand to protect against strikes is called *sansho-yoke*. (Figure 1-18) You may feel that this is hard to handle. However, the moment they try to execute a *waza* is very clear. Anticipate

Figure 1-16 *Sei-nitō kote* strike against *gyaku-nitō*.

and hold down at the beginning of their attacking movement (*okori*) with the *shōtō*, or do *tsuki* with the *daitō* at the moment they raise their arms. Otherwise, strike left *kote* (Figure 1-19) or *tsuki* (Figure 1-20) when they raise their arms. This should not be a problem for orthodox *nitō*.

Figure 1-18 *sansho-yoke*

Figure 1-20 *Gyaku-nitō tsuki* against *sansho-yoke*.

• **Open Type**

The difficulty of this type is working out what path the *shinai* will take. (Figure 1-21) Use *ichi-monji-no-kamae* to limit the possible paths the attacking *shinai* can take. (Figure 1-22) Then let them strike and draw them out. When attacking with the *shōtō*, the opponent will focus on the *shōtō* unconsciously, so aim and strike at this moment.

Figure 1-19 *Gyaku-nitō hidari-kote* against *sansho-yoke*.

Figure 1-21 Open *kamae*. Figure 1-22 *ichi-monji-no-kamae* (*gyaku-nitō*)

MARTIAL AIDS

THE SHOE/KOTE DRYER

By Michael Ishimatsu-Prime

I love Christmas, so imagine my delight when I saw on the living room chair—I have not got around to buying a tree in Japan yet—some presents from my wife. Amongst them was a beautifully wrapped box of a decent size that caught my eye.

Thoughts raced through my head as to the delights that could be contained within. Well, I opened the box to find a shoe dryer. I was dumbstruck for a short while, but remembered to say, "Thank you very much. It's great." I could not think of a reason why my wife would buy me a shoe dryer—I did not remember having wet shoes that needed drying. Then I thought, "What if she's dropping hints? Can she smell my shoes? Do my shoes need constant washing therefore justifying the need for a shoe dryer? Can she smell my feet? Do my feet smell? Oh no, if she can smell my feet, then so can my colleagues! When I leave the office, does everyone breathe a sigh of relief?"

Perhaps sensing my confusion, she said, "It's for your *kote*." I am used to being told, as I am sure are most husbands/wives/boyfriends/girlfriends of kendoka, that my *bōgu* smells. I take great care of mine and try to keep it clean as best as I can. After every practice, I wipe the inside of my *men* and *kote* with a wet *tenugui*, spray with antibacterial liquid purchased from the local *bōgu* shop, place on a chair in the spare room, and leave it in front of a fan for a few hours to dry it. However, despite my best efforts, it does develop an odour that we do not really notice, but which non-practitioners find offensive/repulsive/nauseating *etc*.

My old apartment had a large balcony on which I could hang my *bōgu*. It was not in direct sunlight, and did not get wet even in heavy rain, so was a great place to air out my equipment. There is no such place in our new house, and the spare room is now being used. This means that my *men* and *kote* have to be dried in the entrance to the house with my *gi* and *hakama*, which hang nearby on the toilet door frame—a veritable perfect storm of odour. Now, whenever you walk into our house, especially after I have been to *keiko*, you will know that it is the abode of a kendoka. Either that or a tramp, and my wife probably does not want to live with either. Hoping to do something about the smell, she bought me a shoe dryer.

The shoe dryer has a small plastic body with two nozzles that protrude from its top. Wet shoes can be placed over these nozzles that have slits cut into the top through which warm air is blown. *Kote* also fit over them. The heat generated is not strong because leather shoes will shrink a lot if dried quickly. This means that it is perfect for the palms of *kote*. Inserted underneath the nozzles are small bags of charcoal, a material that is known to absorb odours. It also blows out ozone which has odour-eating properties.

There are several attachments that come with the shoe dryer. You can remove the nozzles and replace with two double nozzle attachments making it possible to dry two pairs of *kote* (or shoes) at the same time. It also comes with two accessories for drying boots. These are long, corrugated plastic tubes that can be extended and bent into any shape. I have found this useful for drying my *men*.

When I come back from *keiko*, I wipe and spray my *men* and *kote* in the same way that I did before. However, now I put the *kote* on one of the double attachments, put my *men* back in my *bōgu* bag, and bend the long boot-drying tube into position so that it dries the chin rest part of my *men*. I turn it on at night with the timer, leave it as it is, and in the morning, all I have to do is take my *kote* of the machine, put them in my *bōgu* bag and I am good to go.

I have been using this device for a few months now, and while it may not be making my *kote* and *men* smell better, it certainly is stopping them from getting worse. It is made by Bearmax, and while you might not be able to purchase the same model outside of Japan, there are similar devices for sale online. And just think, if your shoes get wet, you will have something to take care of them, too! Check a shoe dryer out—it will appease a disgruntled spouse, and it may just increase the life of your *bōgu*!

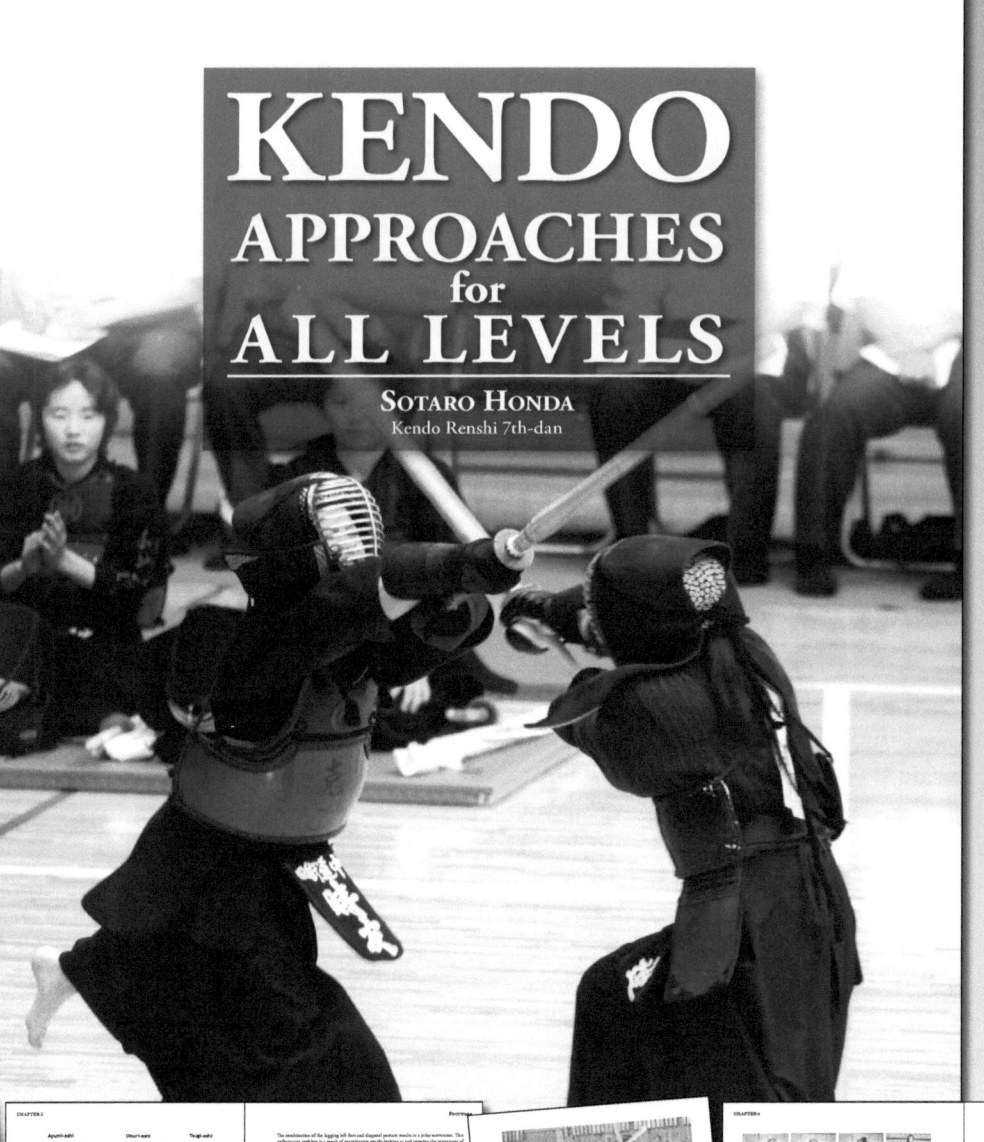

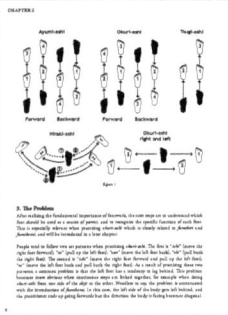
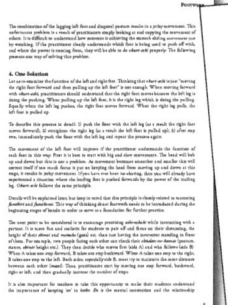

Kendo World is proud to announce our latest publication to enhance your understanding of kendo. Dr. Sotaro Honda (R7-dan), student of H8-dan Masatake Sumi-sensei, has been a longtime contributor to Kendo World, and has spent much of his kendo career helping international kenshi. His latest book is a must have for all practitioners and instructors, and explains various aspects of kendo training in a way that is both accessible and eye-opening. He covers the basics from footwork, to various *keiko* methods such as kakari-geiko and *ji-geiko*, and offers many useful hints for *shiai* strategy. Buy this book on Kindle as a download, or as a hard copy. See **www.kendo-world.com** for more details!

KENDO —Approaches For All Levels— *Sotaro Honda* Kendo Renshi 7-dan
Kindle Edition $7.97   Paperback $22.46

To order, visit **www.kendo-world.com** more information, mail to **info@kendo-world.com**

Published by **BUNKASHA** INTERNATIONAL CORPORATION / 2498-8 Oyumi-chō, Chūōku, Chiba-shi, Chiba, JAPAN 260-0813

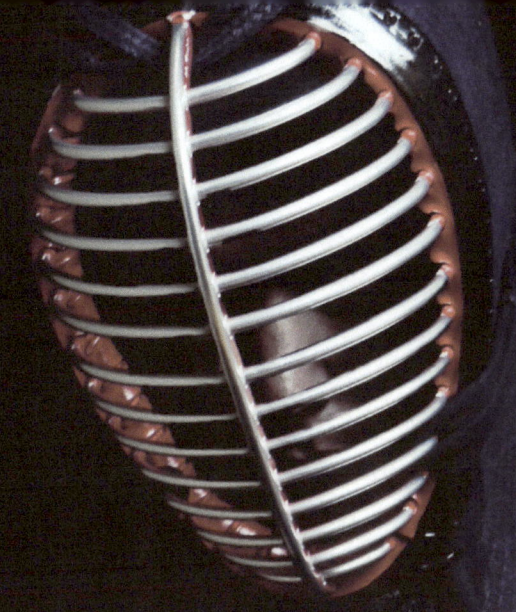

ALL JAPAN BUDOGU
FREE INTERNATIONAL SHIPPING ON ALL ORDERS!

常識を超える
勝利のゴールドマーク

www.alljapanbudogu.com